# LOS ANGELES COUNTY BOULDERING

Matthew Dooley
Dimitrius Fritz
William Leventhal

# LOS ANGELES COUNTY BOULDERING

*by Matthew Dooley, Dimitrius Fritz, and William Leventhal*

K. Daniels & Associates
K. Daniels & Associates has been publishing adventure guides since 1991. Our goal is to create the highest quality guidebooks possible. If you have printing needs, are envisioning an outdoor guide, or are a wholesaler looking to sell our titles, visit our website at kdanielspublishing.com or email us at info@kdanielspublishing.com

Copyright © 2017 K. Daniels & Associates
Copyright © 2017 Matthew Dooley
Copyright © 2017 Dimitrius Fritz
Copyright © 2017 William Leventhal
August 2017

Printed in South Korea
ISBN: 978-0-692-03321-0

Notice of Rights - All rights reserved under the International and Pan-American Copyright Conventions. No part of this book, including maps, photographs and topos, may be reproduced or transmitted in any form or by any means, electronic or mechanical, including photocopying, recording, by any information storage or retrieval system, except as may be expressly permitted by the 1976 Copyright Act, or in writing from the publisher.

Front Cover Photo:
Trevor Seck on a Malibu Creek State Park gem. Photo: Devlin Gandy

Previous Page:
Matthew Dooley on Whirlpool Roof. Photo: Ethan Gia

Layout and Design by Matthew Dooley

### NOTICE OF LIABILITY
The information in this book is distributed on an "as-is" basis, without warranty. While every precaution has been taken to make this guide as accurate as possible, neither the authors nor K. Daniels & Associates shall have any liability to any person with respect to any loss or damage caused by the information contained within this book

### WARNING
Rock climbing is an inherently dangerous sport in which severe injury or death may occur. The user of this book accepts a number of unavoidable risks. It should be assumed that information could be erroneous. Please examine the rock carefully before climbing it. Use your own judgment to determine whether you are up to a particular route or not.

The authors, editors, publishers, distributors, and land owners accept no liability for any injuries incurred from using this book.

## DEDICATIONS/ACKNOWLEDGEMENTS

I want to start off by thanking my mom, she always told me to go for it and so I did, thanks mom! Then I have to thank Matt Dooley for being the motivating factor behind this guidebook because if not for him, I'd still be throwing laptops across my living room. Special thanks to Dale Eckert, who got me into climbing as well as Jeff Johnson and Paul Anderson who made me the climber that I am today. Then there are "The Dudes" (Spencer Church, Sam Eaton, Sara Heart, Bryan Hayes, Chase Baron, Spencer and Austin Josif, Nick "Peach" LeProhon, Eric "Balls Deep" Benevente, Daniel Vakili, Michael Bailey, the B-nomes crew Brandon and Naomi Johnson, Jenna "Panties" Isenberg, Lance Carrera, Jofrann Gonzales and my co-authors Matt and Bill) who are some of the best spotters in the world as well as climbers/people to be around. To John Sherman aka "The Verm", thanks for always being an inspiration you old fucker. Plus a thank you to Larry Epstein for his editing work and all the other people who lent a picture, information or any kind of help. Most of all I want to thank Kevin Daniels for his patience and understanding for my lack of computer skills along with the years of waiting for this guidebook to get done.
- Dimitrius

I want to thank my father, Robert M. Leventhal for all his unwavering support of my interest in climbing over the years. His acceptance of my pursuing climbing in its many forms, allowed me to achieve beyond what I ever dreamed possible and that has shaped my life forever. Thank you. I also want to thank the people who either taught me or showed me new levels of stoke and commitment. Individuals such as Matt Oliphant, Vaino Kodas, Bob Kamps, Herb Laeger, Mike Guardino (aka Guargoyle), John Yablonski, John Long, Banny Root, Jeff Johnson, Dimitrius Fritz, Paul Anderson, Rob Mulligan, John Sherman, Sam Eaton, Mike Matheson and so many others it would take an entire page to list the many folks I've enjoyed great times on the boulders with. In addition, I want to thank the upcoming generation of climbers who will inherit these fields of stone and respect what nature provided to us and to keep it real and proud so that the next generation can look up to their deeds and accomplishments with admiration and perhaps a bit of awe like I have experienced as well, which keeps the fires stoked.
- William

For Archer and Miles. Thanks to my wife, Karrie, for supporting with me throughout this project. Everyone else you know who you are.
- Matt

## In Memory of Bleau

# TABLE OF CONTENTS

FORWARD ..................................................................

INTRODUCTION ..........................................................

GEOLOGY ............................................................... 1

NATIVE LOS ANGELES ................................................ 2

TEMPORAL BOULDERS/SANDBOX ................................. 2

MINIHOLLAND ......................................................... 3

DOOMSDAY BOULDERS .............................................. 4
    LOST KEYS AREA ................................................. 4
    ELEPHANT GRAVEYARD ......................................... 5
    THE HOMESTEAD .................................................. 5

MALIBU CREEK STATE PARK ........................................ 5
    APES WALL ......................................................... 6
    STUMBLING BLOCKS ............................................. 6
    GHETTO WALL ..................................................... 7

TUNNEL BOULDERS ................................................... 8
    UPPER AREA ....................................................... 8
    MAIN AREA ......................................................... 9
    PICNIC AREA ....................................................... 1
    HYPODERMIC AREA .............................................. 1
    DOWN BY THE RIVER ............................................ 1
    SOMETHING IN THE BUSHES ................................... 12

MARTIAN'S LANDING ................................................. 12

STONEY POINT ......................................................... 12
    WEST ................................................................. 1
    SOUTH ............................................................... 1
    EAST .................................................................. 1
    NORTHEAST ....................................................... 1
    NORTH .............................................................. 1
    CANYONS ........................................................... 1
    SUMMIT ............................................................. 1

## PURPLE STONES ... 195
- HEADWATERS ... 198
- HALFWAY BOULDERS ... 202
- MAIN AREA ... 204
- WHIRLPOOL ... 216
- BANNY SECTOR ... 222
- GUERRILLA FIELD ... 224

## THE COBBLESTONES ... 227
- LOWER AREA ... 229
- UPPER AREA ... 236

## TICK ROCK ... 243

## HORSE FLATS ... 249
- ROMEO VOID ... 252
- MAIN AREA EAST ... 254
- MAIN AREA WEST ... 284
- PIE SLICE/TITANIUM MAN ... 298
- TEFLON PRESIDENT ... 301
- TOPROPE WALL ... 304

## INDEX ... 306

# LOS ANGELES COUNTY BOULDERING

## FORWARD *by John "Largo" Long*

We like to consider bouldering a relatively recent invention but in Southern California the sport dates back to 1935, when Glen Dawson and members of the Sierra Club started clawing up the sandstone rocks at Stoney Point, in the San Fernando Valley. Fifteen years later Royal Robbins, and later, most all of the Yosemite pioneers, put weekday sessions in at Stoney, a tradition continued by the great Bob Kamps, and kept alive by countless others, right up to the present day.

When I first started climbing in the early 1970s, a good measure of your technical skill was to visit Stoney (a two hour drive from my hometown in Upland) and get spanked by the great problems that had gone up over the years. A few seasons later we were putting up our new problems and exploring other areas found throughout the canyons, arroyos and mountain ridges spread across greater Los Angeles County.

My normal partners on these exploratory ventures were Richard Harrison and Ricky Accomazzo, who went on to make historic ascents in Yosemite, Canada, Mexico, the Alps, and in Richard's case, to almost single handedly make the Red Rocks a destination area for climbers the world over. We often were joined by John Bachar, one of the finest, and boldest, climbers on the planet throughout the 1970s and '80s. And we all started on the boulders.

Back then, the tradition ("trad") ethic was still in place and while pure difficulty was valued, the accent was on excitement - basically scaring the shit out of yourself every time out - so the promise land was found through ropeless ascents of Stoney classics like the big overhang on Rock 2, Ummagumma, and Yabos Arete, to mention a few. When the action shifted to the Malibu Tunnels, the Purple Stones, and half a dozen other areas, the biggest, steepest, scariest routes were always the principal draw.

Some of my fondest memories are of thrashing down the brushy incline to the Purple Stones and soloing up the big slabs and aretes above gathering lagoons, teeth chattering as we pinched tiny cobbles in the conglomerate rock. Here was freedom. Here was physical art, shared by a brotherhood of like-minded folks who had grown up together. It felt almost illegal that we could have so much fun and squeeze so much satisfaction from such simple pleasures.

I could recite a thousand stories on a thousand different boulders but bouldering is an experience, first and foremost, so the truth is found in the doing. The value of a guidebook like this is that it tells us where lies the gold. LA climbers are lucky to have so many great bouldering gardens all within driving distance, each with a rich heritage and room for creative souls to add to the legacy.

And owning to their rich history, most all of the areas listed herein are legacy areas, much as Stoney Point was a legacy crag with I first climbed there as a sophomore in high school, meeting the gritty sandstone at the juncture of back then and not yet, and pulling for glory right now. Riding old moves into the future. Following the line of phantoms whose bones might well be dust. It seemed like the collected stoke of the many who had come before was engrained in the rock, and murmured to me that all I had to do was make the next move to rub elbows with Glen Dawson, Royal Robbins, Yvon Chouinard, Bob Kamps, John Bachar, and the thousands of others who had made the LA County boulders their own.

# FORWARD

# LOS ANGELES COUNTY BOULDERING

## INTRODUCTION

What you have in your hands is the best bouldering guidebook ever written for the Los Angeles County bouldering areas. The typical climber doesn't think of Los Angeles as a city that has any good bouldering, with most only knowing about Stoney Point, but there's more bouldering in L.A. County than the world knows. From the boulders strewn along creeks near the beach to alpine bouldering above 6,000ft, the diversity of climbing in Los Angeles County is huge. There is so much good climbing all within an hour drive or so from the heart of L.A. All in all Los Angeles County is a great place to climb, blessed with excellent weather and a great variety of rest day fun. From the beaches to the mountains, to restaurants and great nightlife, there is something for every kind of climber, with a variety of rock from granite to sandstone and some volcanic pocket pulling as well. So turn the page and experience what Los Angeles County bouldering has to offer. Some areas have been purposefully left out of this guidebook due to ongoing disputes regarding property lines, access rights, and parking.

## WHEN TO VISIT

Los Angeles is a year round climbing area as it has plenty of sunshine throughout the year and an average of only 35 days with measurable precipitation annually. Regardless of the time of year there's something climbable. Summers can be hot at times but there are places to hide from the heat. We do get some rain during the winter months (yeah even in Los Angeles) but if conditions are right it can dry out in a couple days. All the creek areas get a few feet of rise in water level during the winter months but can still be accessed with ease. The landings just may get slightly worse. The main gate at the entrance of Horse Flats closes November 15th to April 11th but you can still climb there during that time if you don't mind the extra couple miles added to the hike. Fall, spring and winter offer up the best conditions.

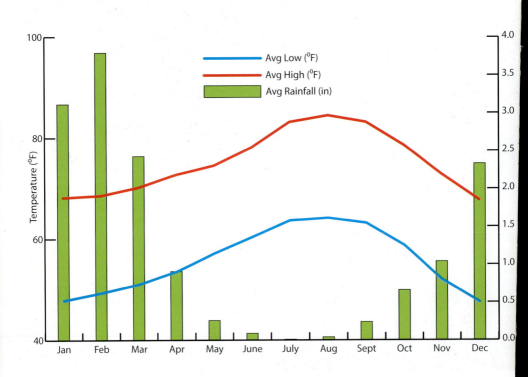

# INTRODUCTION

## GETTING HERE

Los Angeles is a major city accessed from practically any major freeway system in the country. In the age of the internet, putting driving directions in here to help you find Los Angeles seems a bit ridiculous. Just pull out that phone or old road atlas, find Los Angeles, and point your car in the right direction. If you're flying into the area Los Angeles International Airport (LAX) is your best bet. Once you're here you'll find directions at the start of the sections for each climbing area within Los Angeles County. There is a main map on page 18 which shows each area around Los Angeles.

## DANGERS

Poison Oak grows like crazy in the Santa Monica Mountains. If you don't know what it looks like have someone show you that does. You may also stumble upon rattle snakes, mountain lions, bobcats, coyotes, and more. Do not take selfies with any of these things (except maybe the poison oak) if you want to make it out alive. Be aware of your surroundings at all times and if you get the feeling you're being watched by something in the bushes, make some noise. Landings tend to be pretty bad in the Santa Monica Mountains in particular so bring pads and some solid spotters....

A lot of the areas in the Santa Monicas require approaches along busy roads. Keep as far off the side of the road as possible and keep an eye on traffic in order to stay as safe as possible.

You shouldn't be in the areas in the Santa Monicas during or immediately after a rain climbing anyways, but when the rain hits the creeks can rise FAST. Depending on the amount of rain they can be A LOT. Locals can be pretty brutal if you are caught climbing immediately after a rain or spray painting rocks so do your best to avoid doing these things. Don't get ostracized by the community.

*Creek turned river during the rains of winter of 2016/2017. Photo: Devlin Gandy*

## EATS AND SLEEPS

There's no way we came name all of the restaurants in Los Angeles. Just know that no matter what kind of food you're in the mood for after a climb, there's a place that will have it. When it comes to camping in Los Angeles there's a few options. Malibu Creek State Park (MCSP), Leo Carillo, and Pt. Mugu all offer camping at a steep price. MCSP you'll likely have a much easier time finding a site as Leo Carillo and Pt. Mugu tend to fill up months in advance. If you've got a truck or van though, you can pretty much "camp" out anywhere along the Pacific Coast Highway alongside a bunch of surf vans. Horse Flats has camping available on a first come first serve basis from early April to early November at $12.00 a night/day.

## REST DAYS

It's not what you can do, it's what can't you do in Los Angeles. Enjoy the beaches, snowboard in the local mountains, go to Hollywood to see the stars, hit up countless museums. Basically there's bars, restaurants, concerts, amusement parks etc. There's also hundreds of hikes and mountain bike trails all around L.A. to keep you fit. Use the internet. That's what it's there for.

## ETHICS

> ### DO NOT CLIMB ON SANDSTONE FOR A MINIMUM OF 48 -72 HOURS AFTER A RAIN.

No matter how long it's been since you've climbed or how close you were to completing your project right before the rain started, let's give things the proper time to dry so they're around for as long as possible. We've got some really sensitive rock in the Santa Monica Mountains and we need to do what we can to protect our limited resources so we can continue to enjoy them for years to come. This isn't to say that if you climb only on super dry days that nothing will ever break on you, but climbing on things while they're still wet will only accelerate the degradation. **As a general rule of thumb, stay off the rock for about 3 to 5 days after a rain depending on the weather following the rain. Cold and cloudy means you'll be closer to that 5 day mark while sunny and warm will put you closer to the 3 day mark.** This is actually a good guideline to apply to your sandstone adventures regardless of whether it's here in the Santa Monicas or elsewhere. It's not that difficult. Rainy days (and the days following) are why we have climbing gyms. Horse Flats is the only granite area detailed in this guide. If you can't stand the thought of heading to the gym head there instead of breaking holds somewhere else.

Outside of that, no chipping, chiseling or gluing on any rock in any area and NO wire brushing on the sandstone!! Please clean up your tick marks, KOOKS, you know who you are! Keep it pure and the rock clean to make the visit nice for the next climber. Basically respect the rock and clean up after yourself.

Camping is not allowed down in the creeks so don't jeopardize access for everyone else to save yourself a few bucks. Just camp out at Malibu Creek State Park or somewhere free along Pacific Coast Highway. Please refrain from fishing in the stream as it is home to endangered steelhead trout. Pack out any trash you bring in (and gain some points for packing out trash that you find that isn't yours). Let's keep this little oasis as clean as we can

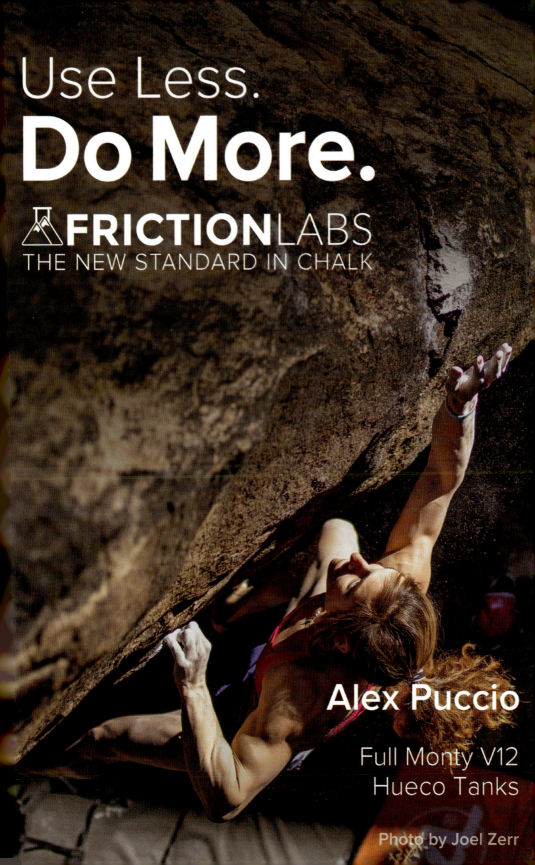

## ETHICS (CONTINUED)

Just in case you forgot. We don't care if you're a pro climber visiting the area for the first time...

# *DO NOT CLIMB ON SANDSTONE FOR A MINIMUM OF 48-72 HOURS AFTER A RAIN*

## HOW TO USE THIS GUIDE

This guidebook is divided into sections starting from the west to the east of the county. All areas have maps and detailed directions which show parking and the layouts of the areas as well as details on approaches and driving directions. The maps here are just for reference and certainly don't capture every aspect of the landscape. In the canyons especially landscapes change drastically from season to season depending on the amount of rain. You've used a guide book before probably and you'll likely just skip over this section anyways, but a sample map is shown below to give you the general feel for things.

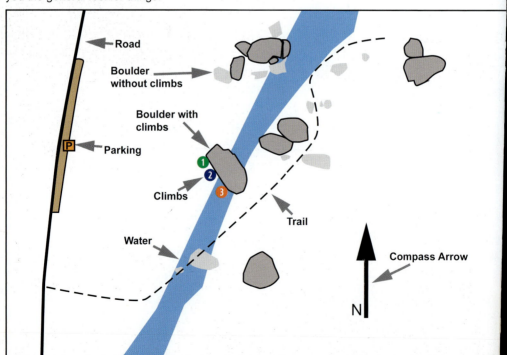

# Your choice...

New stainless steel bolt rated to 8000 lbs or more...

...or old 1/4" bolt with recalled Leeper hanger.

Help us replace old bolts with top-quality stainless steel bolts. The American Safe Climbing Association has helped replace over 15,000 bolts throughout the country. Donate today to help us replace old bolts!

www.safeclimbing.org

The ASCA is a 501(c)3 organization and donations are tax deductible.

# INTRODUCTION

## GRADES/RATINGS

The star rating system is no stars to three stars with only the classics having three stars and being "must do" problems. That being said, even the problems with no stars are decent problems but if you're only there for a short time try and stick to problems with stars. The V-system is used as the grading scale in this guidebook. The V-scale was developed by John "The Verm" Sherman and is most commonly used in America to relate the difficulty of bouldering problems. A "V" precedes numbers in this grading scale. The Fontainebleau (or more commonly Font) scale was used to classify the difficulty of bouldering problems in the boulder-strewn forests near the French town of Fontainebleau. The Font scale is now widely used throughout Europe and states as well and is provided here as reference. The grades are color coded as shown below in the table throughout the guide. Route lines and numbers are colored according to this color scheme throughout the guide.

| YDS | V | FONT |
|---|---|---|
| 5.0 - 5.8 | VB | 3 |
| 5.9 - 5.10+ | V0 | 3/4 |
| 5.11a/b | V1 | 5 |
| 5.11b/c | V2 | 5+ |
| 5.11c/d | V3 | 6a |
| 5.12a/b | V4 | 6b |
| 5.12b/c | V5 | 6c |
| 5.12c/d | V6 | 7a/7a+ |
| 5.13a/b | V7 | 7a+/7b |
| 5.13b/c | V8 | 7b/7b+ |
| 5.13c/d | V9 | 7c |
| 5.14a | V10 | 7c+ |
| 5.14b | V11 | 8a |
| 5.14c | V12 | 8a+ |

The grade distribution throughout all of Los Angeles County as recorded in this guidebook is shown below. There's certainly something to be had for all climbers of all abilities. A table which indicates the grade distribution for each area can be found at each area's intro section.

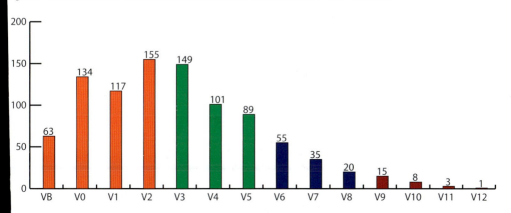

# LOS ANGELES COUNTY BOULDERING

## AREA OVERVIEW

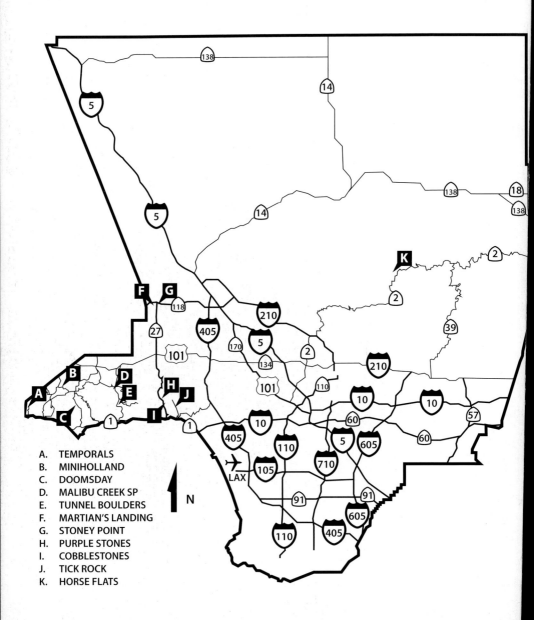

A. TEMPORALS
B. MINIHOLLAND
C. DOOMSDAY
D. MALIBU CREEK SP
E. TUNNEL BOULDERS
F. MARTIAN'S LANDING
G. STONEY POINT
H. PURPLE STONES
I. COBBLESTONES
J. TICK ROCK
K. HORSE FLATS

# LOS ANGELES COUNTY BOULDERING

## LA Geology *by Spencer Church*

The bouldering in the Los Angeles area is diverse in rock type and its geologic past is extremel[y] complex so we will try and keep this fairly basic. The Los Angeles basin is bound on northeast by th[e] San Gabriel Mountains and the Coastal Ranges, namely the Santa Monica Mountains, to the sout[h] west. These mountain ranges and valleys that separate them are part of a larger structure known a[s] the Transverse Ranges. The Transverse Ranges were formed by the movement of the Pacific an[d] North American plates sliding against each other. While the overall movement is nearly parallel to th[e] boundary of the two plates, there are areas where the boundary zigs and zags. These imperfection[s] cause oblique (not parallel but not perpendicular) motion along the plate boundary resulting in area[s] of increased topography. (Take a piece of paper and put one hand flat on each edge and move yo[ur] hands in opposite directions. The paper will fold and raise in parallel ridges that run diagonally. Th[is] is essentially the movements involved in the Transverse Ranges.) The blocks of earth are eroded a[s] they are uplifted and subsequently expose the older underlying rocks.

The San Gabriel Mountains to the north are home to the only "granite" bouldering in the county wi[th] Horse Flats. In geology terms, granite is actually a very specific make up of certain minerals wi[th] defined parameters of percentage of each mineral. Areas like Horse Flats are indeed granite-lik[e] but are more often granodiorite, monzogranite, or other "granitoid" rocks. Climbers will no doubt ref[er] to it as granite, and for all intents and purposes that is essentially what it is. The crystalline rocks [of] the area of Horse Flats were formed deep in the earth's crust during the Mesozoic era (250-65 milli[on] years ago), cooling relatively slowly and allowing the coarse crystals to grow to their large size as w[ell] as develop sharp edges to the crystal that makes grabbing those tiny edges possible yet so taxing [on] the skin. This large body of hardened magma was then uplifted, exposed, and eroded over millio[ns] of years into the landscape you see today.

The Santa Monica Mountains are home to the most diverse climbing in Southern California. T[he] whole range is an anticline (think rainbow shaped) structure that is segmented by many faults. The faults paired with the relatively soft rocks that make up the mountains combine to form very steep a[nd] somewhat loose topography with peaks topping 3000 feet elevation separated by valleys dropping near see level (or to sea level) in just a couple of miles.

The bouldering in the Santa Monica's is mostly on sedimentary rocks with the exceptions of the M[al]ibu Creek State Park boulders, the Dume Boulders and Miniholland which are volcanic. The volca[nic] rocks in the area are referred to as volcanic breccia, which means that as the volcano erupted a[nd] the lava moved up through fissures in the host rock and along the surface it broke apart and took [the] surrounding rocks with it. This is noticeable in the rocks of Malibu Creek especially, where the wa[lls] and boulders present multi colored clasts that have been trapped in the former liquid and now entombed in the walls.

# GEOLOGY

The other areas in the Santa Monica Mountains are sandstones that were deposited in shallow marine environments. The Cobblestone Boulders and Purple Stones in Topanga Canyon offer abundant evidence of the marine deposition with fossilized shells to be found nearby everywhere you look. The Malibu Tunnels Boulders, Temporal Boulders and Sandbox areas also offer fossil evidence of past marine life in the form of both replaced shells and casts of soft bodied creatures. There are also major differences between the Topanga Canyon areas and the other Santa Monica Mountains sandstone areas. The obvious large, mostly rounded cobbles in the Topanga Canyon rocks are drastically different from anything else in the area being most crystalline, granitic rocks not found within many miles of the Santa Monica Mountains. These rocks are evidence of a river that traveled from areas that had granitic rocks to transport via rolling down a stream bed to the point they were rounded like the infamous Lodestone at the Purple Stones. These Cenozoic aged (65-24 million years) marine sandstones were all uplifted and deformed during the same time period that the San Gabriel Mountains did the same.

Stoney Point is situated at the northeast corner of the San Fernando Valley. The rock in this area is known as the Chatsworth Formation, an impressively thick (6000 feet!) late Cretaceous (70-75 million year old) sandstone that formed in a shallow to deep marine environment. The rock at Stoney Point is coarse sand, silt, and occasional small gravel which lend to the abrasive nature of the climbing. This combination of characteristics comes from the underwater landslides and subsequent settling of the dust left behind after one of these "turbidity currents" takes place. One can observe the layers of silt that settle on top after these currents move sediment along the ocean floor preserved in the rock. The Powerglide wall has one of these layers running along the middle of it, creating the horizontal weakness used as hand holds on all the problems on the wall.

Overall, the complex and diverse geologic history of the Los Angeles County area has blessed the climbers of the region with many unique areas. From rocks with igneous origins, both intrusive and extrusive, to sedimentary rocks that were deposited on the floors of the Pacific Ocean. From 5,000 feet in elevation at Horse Flats to the Dume Boulders with the ocean waves crashing along side, Los Angeles climbers and visitors from all over have a unique opportunity to escape the urban hustle and bustle, to make a short drive in almost any direction, at almost any time of year and find sanctuary among the boulders.

# Climbing on Sacred Grounds:
## Sacred Spaces, Cultural Heritage, and Ethical Climbing
*by Devlin Gandy*

At the time of European contact, California was a remarkably culturally and ethnically diverse region—similar in many regards to what we know it as today. Roughly 100 languages, with innumerable dialects were spoken by an even larger number of tribes. Los Angeles country was divided between speakers of Chumashan languages to the West, and Uto-Aztecan speakers to the East and North with Topanga Canyon and the Western end of the San Fernando Valley generally being thought of as a porous boundary line. It was an area of cultural mixing and diversity, with fluid boundaries and strong bustling trade and exchange networks that connected the tribes in LA county to Northern California, the Northwest, Southwest, Great Basin, and Mexico.

The tribes that spoke different but related Uto-Aztecan languages came to be known as the Fernandeño, Gabrielino, Serrano, Tataviam, and Vanyume. I say "came to be known" as through conquest many tribal identities were lost, merged, and reformatted, disrupting tribal identities that had existed for potentially thousands of years—while creating new identities in the process. In many cases, we no longer know the names these people had for themselves because their cultural knowledge and language was forcibly taken away from them. In the wake of such extreme loss, Native Californians have often been referred to by the mission that they were forcefully moved into. For example, the Uto-Aztecan speaking people from the dozens of villages in Los Angeles County become known as Gabrielino, after being missionized at Mission San Gabriel Arcángel.

Contrary to what is taught in 4th grade classes across the state of California, Spanish colonialism was not a positive experience for Native Californians. Native people rarely went willingly into

---

[1] Uto-Aztecan is a Native American language family found in Northern Mexico and much of the Western United States. It includes many tribes in the LA area, as well as more commonly known tribes like the Hopi, Comanche, Shoshone, Tarahumara, and Aztec.

mission system; instead, through systematic violence, kidnapping, destruction of natural resources, breaking of alliances, false promises, and the ongoing effects of European disease, Native Californians were left with little choice but to join the mission community. Within the mission system, traditional knowledge and Native language were often banned as a means to accelerate colonization. In 1834, Mexico secularized the California missions, effectively cutting off what little support the Native Californian mission community had been forced to be reliant upon. Though suddenly free to leave, Native people were typically left will little possessions, no land, and few rights. This situation became far worse in 1850 with California statehood.

Under the guise of Manifest Destiny, Native lands were forcibly taken across the continent. In California 18 treaties were made with California Indian tribes between 1851 and 1852—including some of the tribes from the greater Los Angeles county. Unfortunately, when these treaties made it to the U.S. Senate, they were never introduced, and therefore never ratified. Again, Native people suddenly found themselves lied to and without possessions, with both their former lands and promised reservation lands forcefully taken from them. In the following years, the state of California legalized hunting Native Californians as a legally sanctioned genocide, with newspaper headlines proudly proclaiming massacres of Native Californians on a monthly basis. Just imagine it, you as a Native person surviving the mission system, adopting Western dress and language, surviving the hardships of Mexican California, only to be killed indiscriminately by Anglo-American settlers—it's horrific, and it happened.

In the subsequent decades, when Native people had become visibly absent on the "frontier", the Anglo-American imagination came to idolize Native people. It's an idolization that continues to this day, whether in New Age beliefs, or Coachella fashion apparel, but it does nothing to show respect or consideration for Native people, it simply takes more from them.

Now, you may be asking yourself, how does this history apply to climbing? It is the result of this colonial history of genocide and erasure that there are "wildernesses" to explore, that we find empty and uninhabited places with some cool unknown blocs to get first ascents of. It's because of this history of genocide and erasure that climbers need to be conscientious of the spaces they are exploring, experiencing, and enjoying—because these lands are neither wild nor unexplored, it's just the memories of them have been forcefully taken.

These are all facts I came to learn as a climber seeking new rocks to climb. And if you're like me, and searching for new climbs, you might run into Native spaces, and occasionally sacred spaces. This is something no one mentioned when I started climbing in LA, but something I've come to know well. What might make you realize you're in a Native space? Pieces of shell on cave floors, smoke blackened roofs, artifacts (such as arrowheads), bedrock mortars, and rock art are all clear indications. Much like a church, or a synagogue, these places deserve basic respect and consideration—not only for the place itself, but for the people still connected to it.

To disambiguate a little bit before moving on, there are two primary ways people discuss the cultural places and materials left by Native people. These are from an archaeological perspective and a Native perspective, which though distinct, can be complementary. Legally speaking, Native American places, such as caves with leftover shells from a meal eaten 400 years ago, or an arrowhead in a field, are identified as an "archeological resource" and protected by both local, county, state and federal laws—they are considered as part of our cumulative American cultural heritage. Of course, this perspective continues the legacy of Manifest Destiny, by forcefully possessing sites Native people have had intimate connection to for thousands of years. It also emphasizes that present Native people are disconnected from their own past and cultural landscape. Another way to discuss these sites, which is gaining more legal strength, is as Native spaces. That is, we are not arbitrarily distinguishing these Native American sites as before and after Europeans colonized the area, we are instead acknowledging the continuous connection Native people have to these places.

Known as *'alaxulux'en* in the Barbareño Chumash language, Chumash Painted Cave in Santa Barbara is an exceptional example of local rock art. Unfortunately, by the 1920's, the site had been so vandalized by tourists carving into the paintings that a gate was erected at the entrance. Likely, without that gate these paintings would have been completely destroyed

Generally speaking, Native American's practiced a spatial conception of history rather than a linear time based conception of history. That means where things happened was often more significant than exactly when they happened. Keith Basso described this concept well in his book, Wisdom Sits in Places

> For Indian men and women, the past lies embedded in features of the earth—in canyon and lakes, mountains and arroyos, rocks and vacant fields—which together endow their lands with multiple forms of significance that reach into their lives and shape the ways they think. Knowledge of place is therefore closely linked to knowledge of the self, to grasping one's position in the larger scheme of things, including one's own community, and to securing a confident sense of who one is as a person.

It's in this context that we as climbers need to consider the possible sanctity of rocks, caves, outcrops and landscape features. These might be an ancestor, or a figure in an oral story, or a remnant of creation, the landscape holds the cumulative wisdom and memories of past generations, and these aspects of a rock or outcrop may not be obvious. In many cases, these remote places are some of the last protected direct and undamaged links Native people have to their own culture and history. It is precisely for these reasons that we as climbers need to be considerate and cognizant of our actions, and realize that we don't need to climb everything, that there is a power, beauty, and history to these places that needs respect, admiration, and consideration. Keep that in mind as you explore the mountains

# NATIVE LOS ANGELES

In writing this, I have spoken with tribal representatives and Native persons descended from the area covered in this guidebook. Unanimously, they ask for their rock art sites and cave dwellings to be left alone, but no particular rock (without obvious signs of human habitation and use [i.e. smoke blackening, rock art, etc.]) has been identified as off limits.

Pictographs defaced by chiseling. Image on the right has been processed with false colorization to highlight faded elements

From my own experiences climbing in the Santa Monica Mountains, I've unintentionally stumbled upon a number of archeological sites, and some sacred sites while out looking for rocks to climb. Generally speaking, I think I was often the first person to see them, but, in one unfortunate case in Topanga, I certainly wasn't the first. The cave was large, with sandy questionable sandstone. The ceiling and walls were smoke-blackened—obvious signs people had been there before. On the back wall, was a panel of rock art, black geometric elements carefully painted—with a chiseled handhold cut right through them. A climber had decided to climb this chossy cave, not satisfied simply with the choss, they chiseled over 30 handholds into the walls—destroying the rock art that was there. Now, I doubt they realized what they destroyed art that was potentially thousands of years old that day. Still, it goes without saying that chiseling is not acceptable anywhere in Los Angeles County, and that if the cave looks like it's been used, leave it be.

Legally speaking, Native American sites are considered both archaeological sites and tribal cultural properties, they federally protected under the Antiquities Act (on federal lands) as well as numerous state and local ordinances (on public lands). In the State of California, additional laws protect both rock art and caves. In terms of the areas in this guidebook, it is illegal to take any Native American artifact (including arrowheads) from any of the areas mentioned in this guidebook. It is also illegal to damage any caves under California Penal Code Part I Title 14 § 623. Any person on State property who intentionally and knowingly breaks, carves, damages, paints, defaces, mars a cave wall; kills or harms plant an animal life in a cave, or has a fire in a cave "is guilty of a misdemeanor punishable by imprisonment in the county jail not exceeding one year, or by a fine not exceeding one thousand dollars ($1,000), or by both such fine and imprisonment".

If you do happen to find rock art or artifacts, here's a simple check list:

Do Not

- Do appreciate, enjoy, take a moment to think of how the world has changed.
- Do contact one of the agencies below if you think the site may be unrecorded, has signs of vandalism, or is being looted (i.e. someone has recently dug holes in the ground).
- Do practice Leave No Trace

- Do not touch rock art.
- Do not climb on a rock that has rock art.
- Do not dig/kick up artifacts
- Do not collect or move around artifacts.
- Do not take artifacts home.
- **<u>DO NOT POST PHOTOS TO SOCIAL MEDIA ACCOUNTS</u>**

# LOS ANGELES COUNTY BOULDERING

Let me emphasize again, do not post photos to social media accounts. To post a site to social media often assures vandalism and desecration—and though it may be something interesting and cool to you, not everyone is going to share your appreciation and respect.

Lastly, archaeology is a science that relies on context. That is, how things are associated by how they were left. So, if you do find something, do leave it there, and if you feel it is significant, notify the local authorities. Below are the general numbers for State and National Parks in the LA area. When you call, let them know about what you're calling about and that you'd like to talk to a park archaeologist.

Los Angeles District State Parks: 818-880-0363

Santa Monica Mountain National Recreation Area: 805-370-2300

These are general numbers for the park, so let them know about what you're calling about and that you'd like to talk to a park archaeologist.

Places to Visit on a Rest Day:

**Autry Museum of the American West**
4700 Western Heritage Way, - Griffith Park, Los Angeles, CA 90027
(323) 667-2000
https://theautry.org

**Chumash Indian Museum**
3290 Lang Ranch Pkwy, Thousand Oaks, CA 91362
(805) 492-8076

**Haramokngna American Indian Cultural Center**
Forest Rte 2N24, Azusa, CA 91702
(626) 449-8975
http://www.haramokngna.org

**Kuruvungna Springs Cultural Center & Museum**
1439 S Barrington Avenue Los Angeles, CA 90025
(310) 806-2418
http://gabrielinosprings.com/

**Satwiwa Native American Indian Cultural Center**
4126 1/2 W Potrero Rd, Newbury Park, CA 91320
(805) 375-1930
https://www.nps.gov/samo/planyourvisit/rsvsatwiwa.htm

Cragside Reading:

- ***The Chumash World at European Contact: Power, Trade, and Feasting among Complex Hunter-gatherers***, by Lynn H. Gamble. Berkeley: University of California, 2008.
- ***The First Angelinos: The Gabrielino Indians of Los Angeles,*** by William McCawley. Ballena Press, 1996.
- ***Bury My Heart at Wounded Knee: An Indian History of the American West***, by Dee Brown. Picador, 2010.
- ***Wisdom Sits in Places***, by Keith Basso. University of New Mexico Press, 1996.

# TEMPORAL BOULDERS

# LOS ANGELES COUNTY BOULDERING

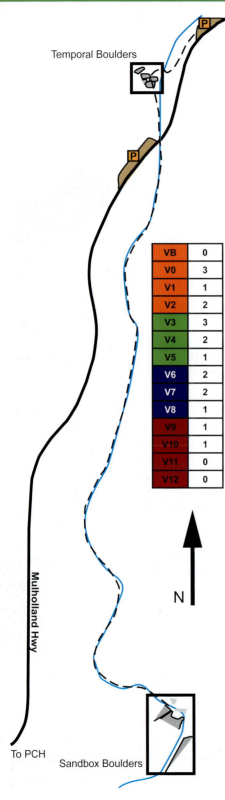

| Grade | Count |
|---|---|
| VB | 0 |
| V0 | 3 |
| V1 | 1 |
| V2 | 2 |
| V3 | 3 |
| V4 | 2 |
| V5 | 1 |
| V6 | 2 |
| V7 | 2 |
| V8 | 1 |
| V9 | 1 |
| V10 | 1 |
| V11 | 0 |
| V12 | 0 |

## Overview
The Temporal Boulders are a small cluster of boulders found off of Mulholland Hwy just a little ways north of Leo Carrillo State Park. The rock is river washed sandstone with odd edges and honeycomb features on decent sized boulders. A quiet little creek bed makes for a nice setting amongst the boulders even though you're only 50ft from the road. The area offers very limited bouldering but the lines are mostly quality. The Sandbox area offers up an amazing 120' traverse on some of the best rock in the Santa Monica's, along with a handful of up problems. The area can be home to swarms of biting black flies in the summer time, so beware!

## History
The Sandbox was discovered by Russell Ericson back in the late 1980's. The Temporal boulders were not found, despite the boulders being able to be seen from the road, until Devlin Gandy came across them in 2005. The area lay dormant until 4 years later when Devlin, Adam Alsadery, and Michael Womack started cleaning the area of dead deer and poison oak. Devlin and the crew then fought through swarms of black flies while developing the lines here. Further activity has yielded a few more offerings in recent years such as Swig's Alcove, which was developed by Matt Dooley and Wil Sterner in early 2014.

## Driving
The Temporals are located just north of Leo Carrillo State Park. If arriving from the south, drive North from Pacific Coast Highway along Mulholland Hwy for ~1.5 miles at which point the stream will cross under the bridge. Parking is on the west side of the road just north of the guardrail. Parking here is VERY limited so if the parking is full, find somewhere else to go. If arriving from the north, take the CA-23S/Westlake Blvd off of the 101. Drive south along CA-23 for 7.1 miles at which point you will make a slight right onto Mulholland Hwy. Continue on Mulholland Hwy for another 5.8 miles to get to the boulders.

## Approach
The Temporals are literally a stones throw from the road. After parking at the guardrail, walk south along the side of the road for ~50 ft at which point you can look down into the streambed and see the boulders. The Sandbox/Alcove area is roughly 15 minutes downstream from the parking by the Temporal Boulders or a 10-15 minute walk from the northernmost area of Leo Carrillo if you happen to be camping there. Keep walking even if you think you should have gotten there already. You'll definitely know when you see it.

# TEMPORAL BOULDERS

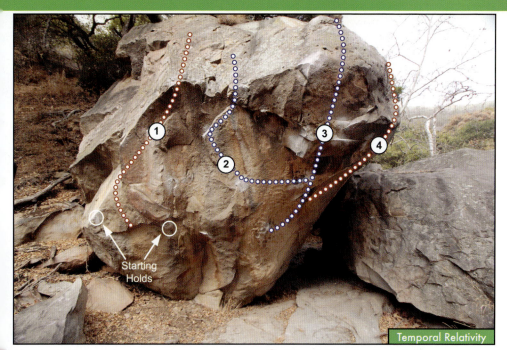

Temporal Relativity

**Torosa - V9** ★
Start left hand on arete and right hand on sharp undercling/sidepull tooth. Slap up the blunt arete trending right and up to flat jugs on top.

**Black Fly Hell - V8** ★ ★
Start sitting on the lowest honeycomb feature on the face. Climb up and left past a small edge to a sloper out left and small crimps at the lip.

**Temporal Relativity - V6** ★ ★
Start same as #2 but head directly up via pockets and crimps to a slopey topout. A lower start down and right bumps the difficulty up a couple notches.

**Attack of The Ants - V10** ★
Start as per Temporal Relativity but instead of bending out to the left arete, head right through heinous sloper and then bad edges and committing moves to the top.

**Uncertainty Principle - V7**
Starts on a shield-esque feature with a funky heel hook to start. Climb up through a few moves to the top.

**Lord of the Flies - V3**
Squat start on a left edge at head height and a right crimp. Climb the overhanging face up out edges to jugs avoiding the elbow break-block.

**⑦ Why Follow the Fox - V0**
Sit start under block and pull up and over lip on blocky holds.

**⑧ ...and the Battle Begun - V2**
Start on opposing sloping sidepulls on the point and squeeze your way through a few moves before continuing to the top.

**⑨ Earthworm Jim - V3**
Sit start on the lower right side of the boulder in the hole on good edges. Trend up and left as far as you can before turning the lip. Can be done with a direct finish after the first couple of moves.

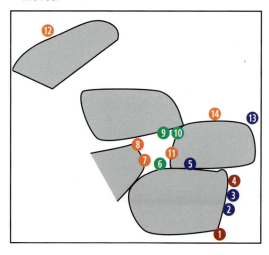

29

# LOS ANGELES COUNTY BOULDERING

Spencer Church on the First Ascent of Black Fly Hell. Photo: Devlin Gandy

# TEMPORAL BOULDERS

Lord of the Flies

**❸ The Waiting - V7 ★**
Starts right hand on a sloping edge and a small undercling for the left. Big move up and left to a block leads to easier climbing through edges up and right to the boulder's apex.

**❹ Unicorn Paradise - V0**
Climb the face via good holds. Many options are available on this wall. Traverse goes at around V2.

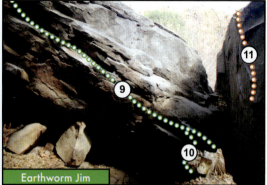

Earthworm Jim

**Crawl Space - V4**
you're small enough you can start even lower an Earthworm Jim way down in the hole on a alactite feature.

**Life Is Short - V2**
imb the lowball face via crimps.

**Digging For Worms - V1**
art at the lowest part of the sloping lip and averse up along the hillside.

Digging For Worms

The Waiting

31

# LOS ANGELES COUNTY BOULDERING

*Wil Sterner on Lord of the Flies. Photo: Matthew Dooley*

# THE SANDBOX

The Sandbox area is located approximately 15 minutes downstream of the main Temporals area. You will come across Swig's Alcove on the west side of the stream first. The Sandbox Traverse is located 100 feet further.

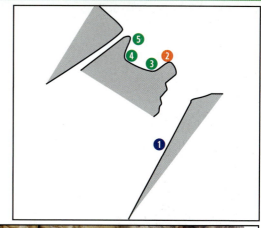

**① The Sandbox Traverse - V6 ★ ★ ★**
Starting on the southern end of the overhanging wall, traverse the entire length of the wall using whatever means of trickery you can manage. Can also be done in a north to south fashion. Got it wired? Try it there-and-back.

**② Mantle Problem - V0**
Start at the left side of the Alcove in a water polished seam. Head up through slopers to a mantle.

**③ It's Nyaaat Easy - V5 ★**
Start sitting on an obvious rounded ledge about 4 ft from the ground. Go up the left hand seam before joining the topout of Swig's Alcove.

**④ Swig's Alcove - V3 ★**
Start with a left hand pocket and spine for the right hand. Traverse left to a big hueco before heading straight up through compression moves to the top.

**⑤ The Ankle Grabber - V4**
Same start as Swig's Alcove, but head to the right arete before heading back up along the lip to meet up with the top of Swig's Alcove

Sandbox Traverse

Swig's Alcove

33

# LOS ANGELES COUNTY BOULDERING

## Overview
The Miniholland boulders are a beginner to moderate area and a roadside attraction so to speak. The few boulders here are right off the road and you literally park next to the first boulder. An easy to get to and easy to walk to area makes this perfect for a quick session, especially if you're in the area and you don't have much time. With a couple dozen problems one can make this a one day session if you're so inclined. The climbing is basic pocket pulling with some edges and side pulls thrown in. The rock is a decent volcanic with some loose rock and the landings are all pretty flat.

## History
People have been bouldering here for decades but minimal development has happened and practically no documentation has been done. With several other boulders spread out around the hillside, one with an adventurous spirit could probably develop a few more problems in the area. The best bouldering will be found on boulder #1 and #2. The Captains Corner, a solo highball, can be found down the road and is well worth doing.

## Driving
From the 101 Ventura Fwy head south towards the ocean on Westlake Boulevard (23) for 5.3 miles to Mulholland Hwy. Make a left onto Mulholland and go mile before parking at a dirt pull out on the right hand west side of the road. From Pacific Coast Highway 1 (PCH) head north on Encinal Canyon Rd for 5.1 mile to Decker Rd veering right for another 2.7 miles until you come to the intersection of Westlake Blvd and Mulholland Highway. Make a right and go 1 mile to the dirt pull out on the right hand side of the road.

## Approach
The approach is very simple and is practically non-existent. Get out of your car and you're there for the Roadside Boulder. You will see a trail next to the boulder too which you can take to the other boulders down the hill.

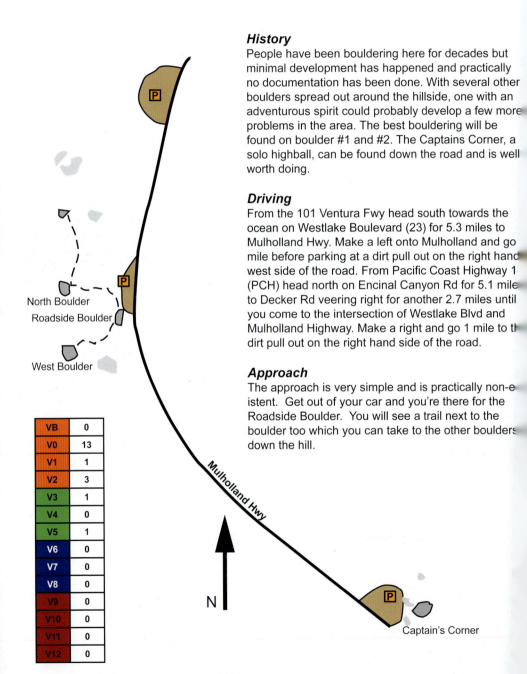

| Grade | Count |
|---|---|
| VB | 0 |
| V0 | 13 |
| V1 | 1 |
| V2 | 3 |
| V3 | 1 |
| V4 | 0 |
| V5 | 1 |
| V6 | 0 |
| V7 | 0 |
| V8 | 0 |
| V9 | 0 |
| V10 | 0 |
| V11 | 0 |
| V12 | 0 |

# MINIHOLLAND

The Roadside Boulder has a TON of variations on the face facing the road.

**Unnamed - V0**
Climb the right arete.

**Unnamed - V0**
Starting about 4 feet left of #1, climb up past the right facing flake feature.

**Unnamed - V0**
Climb the center of the tall face.

**Unnamed - V0**
Climb up to and past the bulge.

**Unnamed - V0**
Climb up the face a few feet to the right of the arete.

**Unnamed - V2**
Climb up the arete from a sit.

**Unnamed - V0**
Climb up the face just left of the arete.

**Roadside Traverse - V3**
Start sitting at the lowest point of the boulder, traverse up and around the corner to the tallest point of the face.

**Unnamed - V0**
Climb the arete from a sit start at big jugs.

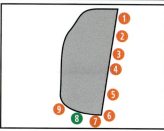

37

Colin Rosemont on a Miniholland classic  Photo: Joshua Roth

# LOS ANGELES COUNTY BOULDERING

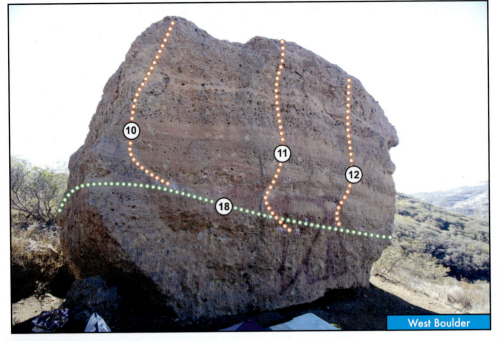

West Boulder

West Boulder

**10 Unnamed - V0**
Climb the northwest corner from a stand start.

**11 Unnamed - V2**
Climb the center of the face starting on a good left hand sidepull.

**12 Unnamed - V2**
Climb the face via sharp pockets.

**13 Unnamed - V1**
Climb the arete from a sit start to finish directly above the little alcove.

**14 Unnamed - V0**
Climb up on good pockets/edges. This is also the downclimb.

**15 Unnamed - V0**
Climb just to the left of the arete.

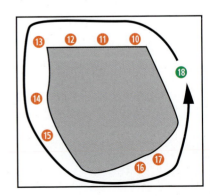

# MINIHOLLAND

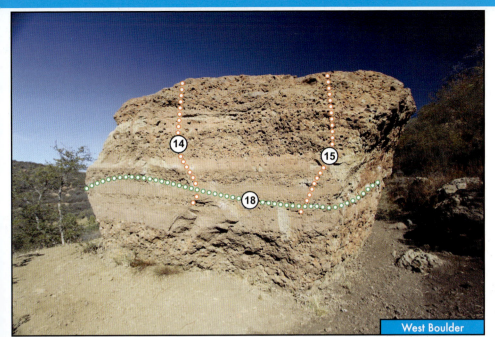

West Boulder

**Unnamed - V0**
Climb the overhanging face trending left from good edges.

**Unnamed - V0**
Climb the overhanging face trending right from good edges.

**Miniholland Traverse - V5**
Traverses the full boulder. Doesn't matter where you start or what direction you go.

The other boulders on the hillside have become overgrown and have been left out of this guidebook. These boulders are host to a few good warnups but nothing spectacular. The Captain's Corner Boulder is down the road about a quarter mile east and is much more deserving of your time if you're in the area.

**19 Captain's Corner - V0 ★**
Climb the highball arete.

West Boulder

41

# DOOMSDAY BOULDERS

# LOS ANGELES COUNTY BOULDERING

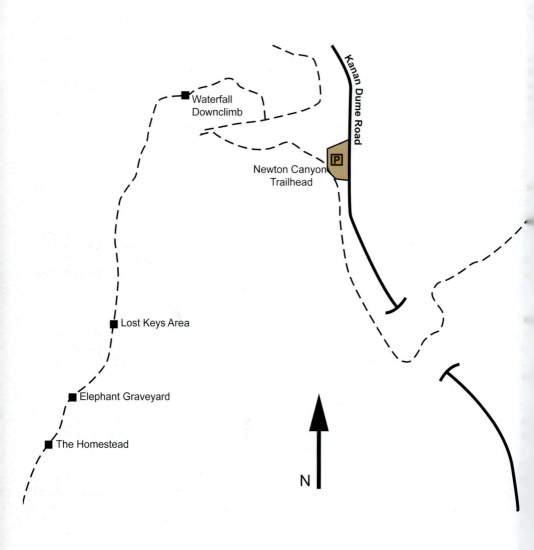

| VB | V0 | V1 | V2 | V3 | V4 | V5 | V6 | V7 | V8 | V9 | V10 | V11 |
|----|----|----|----|----|----|----|----|----|----|----|-----|-----|
| 0  | 3  | 8  | 4  | 3  | 3  | 3  | 1  | 0  | 0  | 0  | 0   | 0   |

# DOOMSDAY BOULDERS

## Overview
The Doomsday boulders are a small collection of boulders located in a dry streambed in upper Zuma Canyon. The rock is quality water polished sandstone and is likely inaccessible or underwater after a good rain or when there isn't a drought. The length of the canyon has been hiked and several concentrations of boulders can be found along the way that have not been developed, and are therefore not detailed here. There are definitely still first ascents to be had if you're willing to hike and battle forests of poison oak. With the rains which occurred in the winter of 2016/2017 this area is a practical waterworld with many climbs over or under water and completely unclimbable unless you happen to bring your scuba gear. It is unclear how much of a drought has to be in effect to climb here. Only time will tell. If it's climbable it's well worth a visit.

## History
The summer of 2014 saw southern California amidst one of the worst droughts in recorded history. The complete lack of rainfall turned flowing streams into easily walkable dry creek beds, waterfalls into somewhat sketchy but manageable downclimbs, and receding water levels exposed boulders previously unclimbable unless you were willing to start under 3 feet of water. As bad as the drought was, these conditions made possible the development of at least one new bouldering area within the Santa Monica Mountains National Recreation Area: The Doomsday Boulders. This concentration of boulders, found and developed by Matt Dooley and Brett Morham, holds a plethora of easy to moderate climbs, with a few harder lines thrown into the mix.

## Driving
To get to the Doomsday Boulders, take the Kanan Dume Rd exit from Highway 101 and travel south for ~8 miles until you reach the Backbone Trailhead parking lot on the west side of Kanan Dume Rd. This same parking lot can also be reached by driving north on Kanan Dume Rd from Pacific Coast Highway for ~4.5 miles.

## Approach
Once at the parking lot, pack your bags and beer and head west on the trail. Approximately 5 minutes down the trail you will see a cut trail leading straight down the hillside on the left side of the trail. Take this path, squeezing yourself and your crashpad through some tree tunnels until you are at a stream bed at the bottom. From here follow the streambed downstream for ~20 minutes past a limestone waterfall downclimb and skirting around a pond/waterfall on 3rd class terrain until you get to the first cluster of boulders. If you want to run the approach it should take you around 11 minutes from the parking lot. As mentioned above much of these climbs are now underwater and the approach has sections which now require water traverses to continue downstream unless you want to wade through a forest of poison oak. This isn't to mention the waterfall which is now actually flowing. With that being said, detailed maps have been left out for this particular area outside of the general approach map.

# LOS ANGELES COUNTY BOULDERING

*Brett Morham making the dry waterfall downclimb during the drought. Photo: Matthew Dooley*

Hollowman

# LOST KEYS AREA - DOOMSDAY BOULDERS

The Lost Keys area is the first area that you come across when hiking down and is home to the highest concentration of climbs at the Doomsday Boulders. Hollow Man is ~50 yards upstream from the main area, which starts shortly after passing Barndoor Mafia.

**Hollowman - V1** ❏
Start matched on the lowest crimp rail. Pull to the hollow sloper before gunning to the top.

**Barndoor Mafia - V2** ❏
Starts on a left sidepull and a horrendous right hand sloper. Pull on, control the barndoor, and then climb through slopers to the top.

**Paranoia - V5** ★ ❏
Starts in two pockets underneath the roof. Head out to the arete and up through jugs.

**Slop Arete - V2** ❏
Starts left hand in the diagonal slot in the face and a right hand on the sloping arete. Slap to the arete and then mantle over. SUPER lowball.

Barndoor

Slop/Paranoia

47

# LOS ANGELES COUNTY BOULDERING

Pocket Protector

Lucky Strike

# LOST KEYS AREA - DOOMSDAY BOULDERS

Lost Keys

**Bulletproof Wallets - V3** ★

Starts sitting on a left hand pinch and a right hand pocket. A few moves to crimps leads to a big reach out right to a glorious undercling pocket. Once standing on the ledge midway up, you can press ahead with blatant disregard for your own safety or traverse to the right and downclimb the tree.

**Pocket Protector - V1** ★

Starts matched on a polished block at waist height. Pull through two amazing pockets and finish same as Bulletproof Wallets.

**Lucky Strike - V2**

Start the arete with the right hand split in the bowling ball holes and the left hand on an edge. Climb up through edges and slopers.

**Brett's Arete - V0**

Climb the arete from a sit start.

**Laundryroom Innuendo - V1**

Low start on two pockets. Climb up and right through the pod.

⑩ **Lost Keys Arete - V1** ★

Starts a little stretched out with the left hand on a good pocketed edge and right hand on a low crimp. Fun climbing up the arete.

⑪ **Lost Keys of God - V6** ★ ★

A 20+ move endurance climb which starts squatting on two opposing sidepulls ~3 ft feet apart down inside the cave. Great movement with the only real detractor being the dab potential along the ramp. If you catch it at the right time a god ray shines right into the start cavern.

⑫ **Project**

Starts low on opposing edges. Head up and left through big moves on shallow pockets, a horrid pinch, and sloping edges to a committing and dirty end. Bring a pushbroom.

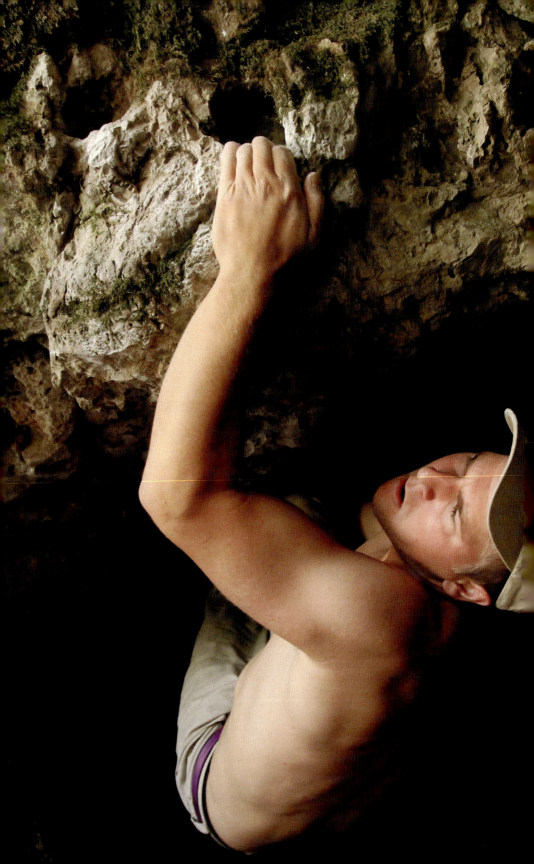

*Brett Morham grabbing an eye socket on Lost Keys of God. Photo: Matthew Dooley*

# LOS ANGELES COUNTY BOULDERING

Monkey Paw

**⑬ Monkey Paw aka Kate Moss - V5**
Start sitting at the arete with the right hand on a block and an edge for the left hand. Traverse up and over out right until you get to a decent sloping rail. Once at the rail, a few short moves will find you standing at the bottom of a very mossy/dirty highball topout.

**⑭ Project**
A direct finish to Monkey paw looks feasible.

**⑮ Neckbeard Aficionado - V2**
Start sitting at the arete and traverse the lip of the boulder. Good movement but inches off the ground. Kind of like that neckbeard being low on your neck when you'd really rather it be filling in on the cheeks. Your mom would be ashamed if she knew you climbed this.

**⑯ Dangermouth - V1**
Starts left hand in a deep mouth and right hand on a vertical pinch. Climbs up and right on water polished holds.

**⑰ Crosshairs - V3 ★**
Starts a couple feet to the right of Dangermouth on a shallow slot for the left hand and a sloper for the right. Go up right to a bad edge before hucking for the lip.

Neckbeard

# LOST KEYS AREA - DOOMSDAY BOULDERS

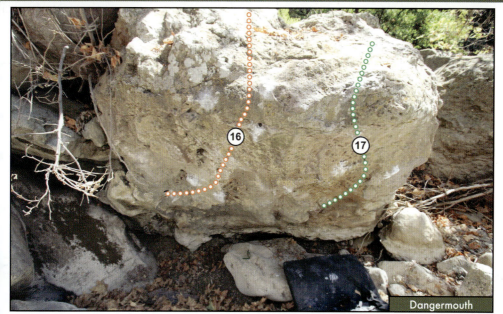

Dangermouth

**Madvilliany - V5** ★ ★

Starts left hand pinching the arete below the obvious water line and right hand on a sloping rock. Move up and left into an undercling before going for the lip.

*Glass Animals is located about 50 yards downstream of Madvilliany*

**19 Glass Animals - V1** ★ ★

Climb the glassy slab on barely there dimples.

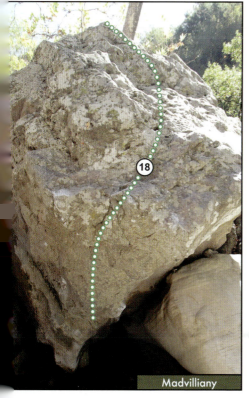

Madvilliany

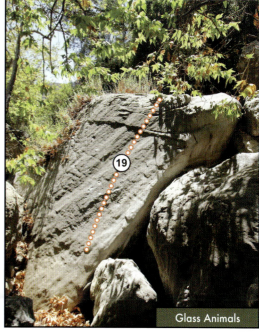

Glass Animals

53

# LOS ANGELES COUNTY BOULDERING

Rafiki's Tomb

The Elephant Graveyard lies a couple hundred yards and a few minutes of hiking downstream from the Lost Keys area. When you find yourself at the top of a wash that opens up where waterfalls should be (or are depending on the season), you're there.

**❶ Rafiki's Tomb - V4 ★**
Stand starting crossed up at a good left hand edge and a bad right hand hold on the bulge from the second tier. Climb up and right through small crimps to a committing move to the lip, An obvious start on edges which face the wrong way at head height at the bottom left of the boulder remains a project. Be careful here, an uncontrolled barndoor could cost you a 10 ft fall down and off a ledge.

**❷ Grip Grand - V4 ★ ★**
Start at the far left/bottom of the sloping ledge at head height. Traverse right to the arete and then slap up the arete to a decent seam before going up to the sloper at the point. Looks scarier than it is and can be well protected as is.

Grip Grand

# ELEPHANT GRAVEYARD - DOOMSDAY BOULDERS

Birds of Prey

**Birds of Prey - V1** ★
tarts at chest height in a pod undercling.
ead up and left through cobble crimps and
opers.

**Grimace - V1**
t start matched in a pod. Follow the pods up
d left.

❺ **Game of Death - V3**
Start on edges at chest height. Make a blind throw around the corner before coming into an undercling in the seam. Continue up along the bulge and seam to the top.

Game of Death

55

# LOS ANGELES COUNTY BOULDERING

Matthew Dooley avoiding the pitfall on Rafiki's Tomb.

# THE HOMESTEAD - DOOMSDAY BOULDERS

The Homestead is located another 5 - 10 minutes downstream of The Elephant Graveyard and contains a few easy climbs along with some remaining projects. The climbs are kind of spread out down this far so just keep hiking. Splitter Choss and Semi-Rad are located 50 yards upstream of Little House on the Prairie, which you can't miss unless you have your eyes closed.

### Splitter Choss - V0 ★
Climbs the perfect hand crack. Climb it up and down 20 times in a row to get your practicing in. The crux is to not giggle uncontrollably.

### Semi-Rad - V0
Climbs the dihedral on the right side of the face.

### Little House on the Prairie - V4
Climbs the arete on the house size boulder for a couple moves on pockets before pulling onto the face and the highball, but low angle, topout. Eventually, the gigantic overhanging face here is choss.

Splitter Choss

Little House

57

# MALIBU CREEK STATE PARK

# LOS ANGELES COUNTY BOULDERING

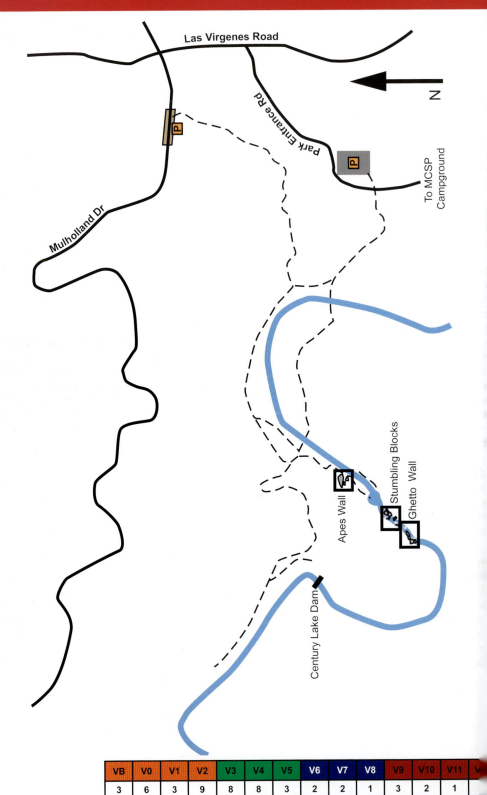

| VB | V0 | V1 | V2 | V3 | V4 | V5 | V6 | V7 | V8 | V9 | V10 | V11 |
|----|----|----|----|----|----|----|----|----|----|----|-----|-----|
| 3  | 6  | 3  | 9  | 8  | 8  | 3  | 2  | 2  | 1  | 3  | 2   | 1   |

# MALIBU CREEK STATE PARK

## Overview

Malibu Creek State Park (MCSP) is known as the set location for numerous movies, television series and commercials. The main top rope wall is named after the infamous Planet of the Apes movie. M*A*S*H was also filmed in the park and several names for problems and cliff bands came from the show. Oscar and Emmy winners have roamed this park for decades taking in its natural beauty and scenery. When the first climbers came they called it little Europe since it reminded them of the Verdon Gorge in France with all the pockets and steep face climbing. The rock is a volcanic breccia with a variety of pockets, edges and cobbles. The rock varies in quality with the best quality rock being down in the creek bed. Bouldering at MCSP favors the intermediate to expert climber since most of the problems have either horrid landings or are over water, not to mention that the most of the boulders are quite high. Dogs are not allowed in MCSP outside of camping/parking areas and must always be on a leash. Best to leave the pooch at home if you're coming here to climb.

## History

Information on early bouldering at MCSP is hard to find. It is not clear when or who first did any bouldering at MCSP. Royal Robbins and Yvon Chouinard were said to be one of the first climbers to go there but there is no documentation of their ascents. Rumors of bad rock and poor landings slowed the discovery to just a few locals for a while. In 1979 Mike Guardino started to develop the bouldering in MCSP along with Mike Paul and Matt Dancey. While not the first, they are believed to be the first to develop the boulders in the creek bed, putting up several of the classic boulder problems like Niagara Fist and Water Hazard. The bouldering surge started in the 80's with many of the classic lines in the park being sent by Mike Guardino, Bill Leventhal and Mike Lechlinski. Lines such as Swim Wear and Lunge or Plunge were sent during this time. In the 90's climbers such as Jeff Johnson, Paul Anderson and Dimitrius Fritz picked up where the others left and added classics of their own such as Evenflow, Recluse Roof, and Yikes! More recently, attention has been focused on on the super steep rock, the most notable ascents being Ivan Green's send of Chubbs in the cave area and Facundo Langbehn's sit start addition to Yikes! in the upper area. The bouldering below the dam area has not been developed much due to high water and bad landings but an adventurous type might be able to find some. The bouldering beyond the Apes Wall is serious and not to be taken lightly, so climb smart and be safe.

## Driving

From the 101 freeway exit on Las Virgenes Road/Malibu Canyon Road, head south for 3.5 miles to the park entrance on the west side of the road. The entrance is just south of Mulholland Hwy. The park entrance can also be reached form the south by driving ~6.1 miles north on Malibu Canyon Rd from PCH. From the entrance, you'll be able to see the kiosk where a day use fee will be collected.

## Approach

From the main parking area inside the park follow Crags road (head west) about 1 mile to the Apes Wall. A little upstream/west from the Apes wall you'll find the rock pool. Skirt around on the south side of the rock pool traversing low on the cliff band to get across to the cave boulder at the main area. Over or through the cave boulder will take you to main Stumbling Blocks area and from here another 5 or 10 minute hike upstream will take you to the Ghetto Wall boulders. A second water traverse is encountered before you reach the Ghetto Wall boulders along the north side of the water.

# LOS ANGELES COUNTY BOULDERING

Apes Wall Traverse

Apes Wall Prow

The Apes Wall area is the first area you'll com across. The boulders and top rope wall are located directly off of the trail to the right

❶ **Planet of the Apes Traverse - V5** ★
Traverse the base of the Apes Wall in either direction. Many variations exits.

❷ **Apes Wall Prow - V2**
Climb the prow up on the hill from a sit start.

❸ **Pai Mei Overhang - V5** ★
Climb the overhanging face.

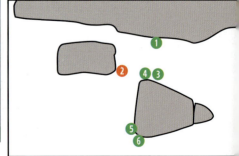

# APES WALL - MALIBU CREEK STATE PARK

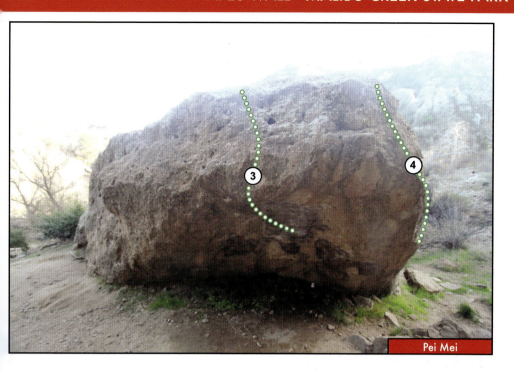

Pei Mei

**Han Shan Arete - V4**
mb the right arete.

**Kuan Chin Roof - V4** ★★
mb the overhang on pockets from a sit start
far back int he cave as you can go

**6  Riceball - V5**
Same start as Kuan Chin but exit out right.

Kuan Chin

63

# LOS ANGELES COUNTY BOULDERING

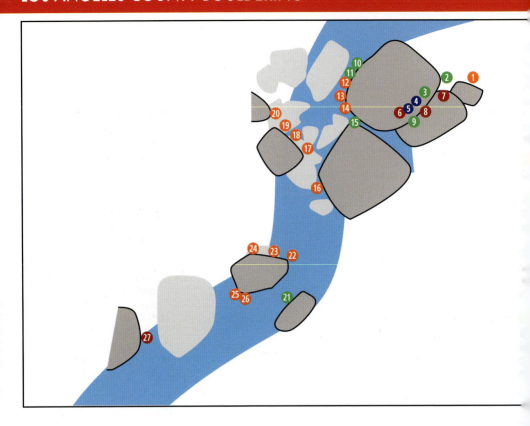

Cave Arete

# STUMBLING BLOCKS - MALIBU CREEK STATE PARK

The Stumbling Blocks Area is located just after the rock pool traverse. Immediately after the traverse you'll come up on a cluster of boulders which form the cave which houses Chubbs and Recluse Roof. The other boulders can be found by scrambling up and over the large boulder or, if the water is low enough, going through the cave to the other side.

### ❶ Warm-up - VB
Climb up face via obvious pockets.

### ❷ Cave Arete - V3 ★ ★
Climb the obvious arete from a stand start on pockets and edges to the apex above the pit.

Climbs 3 through 6 are located on the right hand wall of the cave and climb the overhanging face above a wet landing. Lighting on that wall is always garbage so there's no pictures.

### ❸ Bachar Ladder - V3 ★ ★
Climb up pockets, trending left, to finish at a large jug hueco pocket. Step back onto the boulder behind you from the jug pocket to finish.

### ❹ Cave Direct - V6 ★
Start in a large hueco with a pistol grip inside. Fire up pockets to the same finishing hueco of Bachar Ladder.

### ❺ If You Dare - V7 ★ ★
Start in decent pockets and climb up and right to finish same as Bachar Ladder.

### ❻ Cave Traverse - V10 ★ ★
Traverse left to right along the middle of the wall starting from Cave Arete.

### ❼ V9 Dyno - V9 ★ ★
Start on small pockets and make a blind dyno to good holds. A start from the low rail also seems feasible but has not been linked.

### ❽ The Malibu Roof aka Chubbs - V11 ★ ★ ★
Starts hands matched in pocket and work your way up past a shallow hueco and a pinch before continuing up mono pockets to the top.

### ❾ Recluse Roof - V4 ★ ★ ★
Start in far left hueco and traverse right through huecos to finish up prow on the right side of the wall.

Recluse Roof

# LOS ANGELES COUNTY BOULDERING

South America Face

Unnamed

**⑩ Unnamed - V4 ★**
Climb up pocketed face.

**⑪ Unnamed - V3 ★**
Climb up pocketed face.

**⑫ Unnamed - V2 ★**
Climb up the face to the left of the prow.

**⑬ Prow - V2 ★**
Climb the prow avoiding the jugs out right. Tricky start leads to easier climbing at the top

**⑭ South America Face - VB ★ ★**
Choose your own adventure up the tall face on good edges and pockets. Often toproped (there's a bolted anchor on top) but with a so head this is a great warmup. Many variation exist.

**⑮ Unnamed - V3 ★**
Climb up and over the water trending up and right to finish above the slab.

**⑯ Unnamed - V1 ★ ★**
Depending on water height, start low on the horizontal seam. Climb the overhanging fac via pockets over the water.

# STUMBLING BLOCKS - MALIBU CREEK STATE PARK

Gutterball

**Gutterball Left Face - V0** ❑
imb the left face on creaky edges.

**Gutterball Middle Face - V0 ★** ❑
imb the right face through good sloping pods.
so the downclimb if you don't want to walk
ound the back to get off.

**Gutterball - V2 ★** ❑
art in shallow pockets and go up the blunt
ete to committing moves up high over a
rrible landing.

**Unnamed - VB** ❑
mb the prow to the right of Gutterball from a
nd to finish in a big hole.

Unnamed Prow

# LOS ANGELES COUNTY BOULDERING

Kaptain Traverse

Niagara Fist

# STUMBLING BLOCKS - MALIBU CREEK STATE PARK

**① Kaptain Traverse - V4 ★**
Traverse right to left on pockets.

**② Niagara Fist - V2 ★ ★ ★**
Start at the head high pockets at the shelf. Climb up through large huecos to the top. Classic.

**③ Anderson Problem - V1**
Start in center of the boulder just right of the start of Niagara Fist in a little pit. Climb up the center of the face through pockets.

**④ Niagara Arete - V1**
Start in small pockets and climb up the arete.

**⑤ The Lunker - V0**
Traverse over the water before climbing up good holds through the dihedral.

**⑥ Black Box - V0**
Low water required to climb this unless you want to wade through the water to the start.

**⑦ Evenflow - V9 ★ ★ ★**
Start on the far left of the wall with hands matched on a sidepull pocket. Traverse right through crazy rose moves and straight forward pocket pulling to a strenuous finish.

The Lunker

Evenflow

Lucas Goren on Gutterball Middle Face. Photo: Devlin Gandy

# LOS ANGELES COUNTY BOULDERING

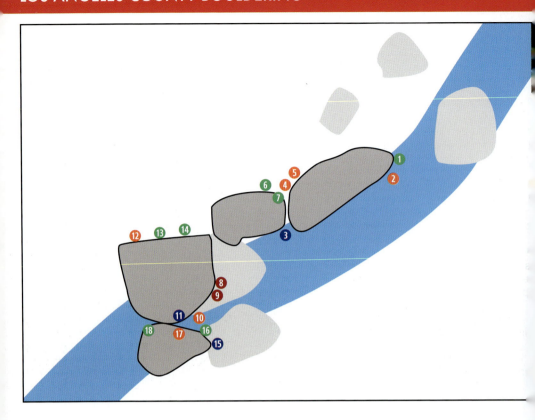

Water Hazard

# GHETTO WALL - MALIBU CREEK STATE PARK

The Ghetto Wall boulders are located ~5 minutes further back in the canyon. You'll have to do another traverse around the base of the wall unless the water level is really low. If you know where the Ghetto Wall is these boulders are located in the stream just past Ghetto Blaster.

**Water Hazard - V3** ★
Start right hand in giant hueco undercling and left hand in pocket. Finish at the apex.

**Traverse or Submerse - V2** ★
Start same as Water Hazard but traverse left around the corner to slab. Keep traversing left to the high point of the boulder.

**Spongebob - V7** ★
As water allows, start as low as possible under the roof and climb up and out the short face to top.

**Unnamed - V0**
Climb the pocketed face trending up and left.

**Unnamed - V0**
Climb the pocketed face.

Spongebob

Warmups

73

# LOS ANGELES COUNTY BOULDERING

**6 Kerwin Problem Right - V3**
Starting under the roof climb out and up the face.

**7 Kerwin Problem Left - V3**
Start same as above but climb out towards the creek and up the face.

**8 Deadfinger - V9**
Originally done as a top rope. Unclear if it's ever seen an unroped ascent.

**9 Huevos - V10 ★**
Start off the boulder to the right of the start for Crank Session or Swim Lesson and climb up and right through small pockets. Finishes right of the big bulge.

**10 Crank Session or Swim Lesson - V2 ★ ★**
Traverse right to left over the water through good holds.

**11 Purple Heart - V6 ★**
Climb out over the water past the purple heart shaped patch.

# GHETTO WALL - MALIBU CREEK STATE PARK

Purple Heart

m Eaton putting on his Swim Wear.  Photo: Matthew Dooley

# LOS ANGELES COUNTY BOULDERING

Powerbeast

Yikes!

76

# GHETTO WALL - MALIBU CREEK STATE PARK

**Celluloid Hero - V2** ★

The right side of the wall. Climb on great pocket holds towards the left of two converging cracks. Finish on big holds straight up.

**Powerbeast - V3** ★ ★

Climb the center of the wall at the green streaks. Climb edges and pockets past the horizontal crack to committing moves up and left to a sloping pocket before finishing through the notch at the lip.

**Thunder Thighs - V4** ★

Climb the left side of the wall to a big move just below the lip off of a small right hand pocket.

**Yikes! - V8** ★ ★ ★

Start hands matched in the bottom of the obvious seam and climb the roof via power moves to a tricky lip turn. A lower start off pockets down and left goes at ~V10.

**16 Whiplash Smile - V4**

Start with a high 2 finger pocket within the smooth band. Jump to mono and climb through ever improving holds to the top.

**17 Swim Wear - V2** ★ ★ ★

Start from the large flat boulder and climb up left to a cantaloupe sized hueco. Use this to gain the lip above.

**18 Lunge or Plunge - V4** ★ ★

Starting off a flat boulder climb up and left up the arete to a big move to a jug. Stick the move or end up in the drink.

Lunge or Plunge

77

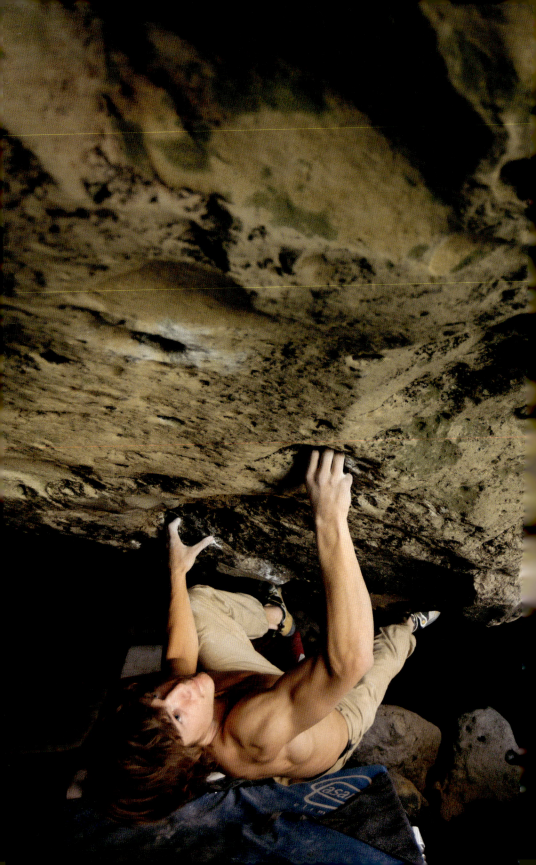

Facundo Langbehn on Yikes! SDS. Photo: Devlin Gandy

# TUNNEL BOULDERS

# LOS ANGELES COUNTY BOULDERING

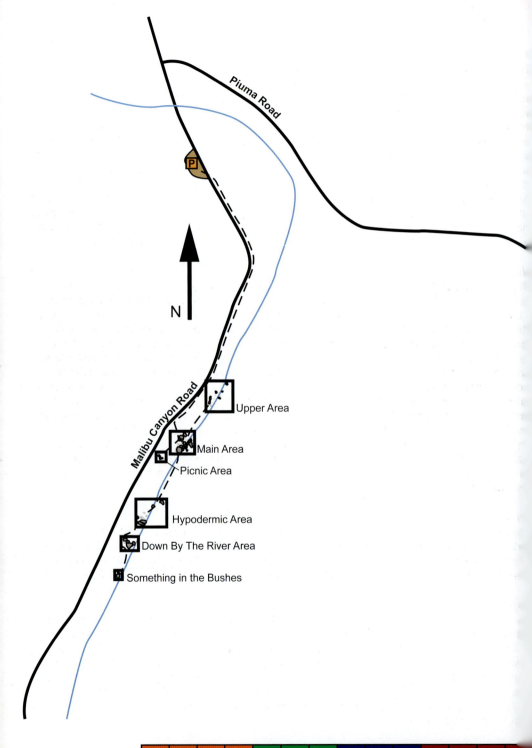

| VB | V0 | V1 | V2 | V3 | V4 | V5 | V6 | V7 | V8 | V9 | V10 | V11 |
|----|----|----|----|----|----|----|----|----|----|----|-----|-----|
| 10 | 14 | 19 | 36 | 33 | 16 | 13 | 13 | 10 | 6  | 4  | 0   | 0   |

# TUNNEL BOULDERS

## Overview

The Tunnel boulders are a year round area in a lush canyon with hundreds of problems on quality rock. The area is best early spring through fall and when L.A. gets sizzling hot during the summer, the Tunnel boulders stay in the 70's to low 80's with a nice ocean breeze making it a great summer spot, although mid-day can be hot in the sun. When Stoney Point is sweltering in the 100-degree heat, the Tunnels will be at least twenty degrees cooler! Early morning or afternoons are best during the summer, with spring, winter and fall being good anytime of day. The rock is water washed sandstone and you'll be surprised about how solid it is. Being water washed for ages has made the rock very solid and makes for great climbing but being sandstone it should still be avoided for a few days after it rains. The area leans towards the intermediate to advanced climber since problems tend to be tall with some bad landings. The beginner climber will have some things to do but will be limited depending on how strong their mental game is. Water gets high during the winter and depending on how much it has rained, can limit the climbing you can access. Plain and simple, the Tunnel Boulders area is well worth a visit for non climbers or climbers of any ability.

## History

Bill Leventhal found the Tunnel boulders on a recon back in 1984 and upon seeing that the rock was solid, knew there was potential for good bouldering. Bill was then part of developing much of the area. To this day he still gets down there for a few sessions. Dave Katz came along shortly afterwards, developing some of the classics like King Pin, Crocodile Rock and Terminator (which was initially done as a top rope). The late 80's also brought in Mike Guardino and Banny Root to the area. They helped in developing some of the area while Leventhal added other classics like Over Lord and Avalon. The area sat relatively dormant through the 90's due to the popularity of sport climbing but a few hard men, like Jeff Johnson, visited from time to time, putting up the now classic, X Problem. In the summer of 2010, Dimitrius Fritz found a half dozen or so boulders just minutes downstream from the main area. With the help of Spencer Church, Devlin Gandy and a few others they developed the lower areas producing another 30 to 40 problems with classics like Hypodermic, Save The Best For Last, and Addiction, a fun highball that would be climbed over a dozen times every day if it were at Stoney Point. In 2015 a few more classics went up such as Binding not Included and Pablo Escobar. These new areas helped make the Tunnels a wonderful destination for climbers of all abilities.

## Driving

From the 101 freeway head south on Las Virgenes Road/Malibu Canyon for ~5.1 miles to the Tapia Park Day Use Area parking lot (Parking fees apply) a couple hundred yards south of Piuma road. This same parking lot can be reached by heading north from PCH on Malibu Canyon Rd for 4.5 miles to the dirt parking area on the southeast corner of Piuma Road and Malibu Canyon.

## Approach

From the parking area head south on Malibu Canyon road for a half mile or so. You'll come to a dirt pullout with a rock outcrop on the east side of the road with a small trailhead just north of the rock outcropping. Drop down the steep, blocky trail, past an Oak tree, and into the creek bed. Heading down stream (south) for 100' will get you to the Malibu Lieback boulder and the rest of the main area. From the main area a 5 to 10 minute walk north/upstream will take you to the Terminator boulders and a 10 to 15 minute walk south/downstream will take you to the Squirrel Head and Down by the River boulders. The Something's in the Bushes boulder is a 5-minute walk south/down stream from Squirrel Head boulder.

# LOS ANGELES COUNTY BOULDERING

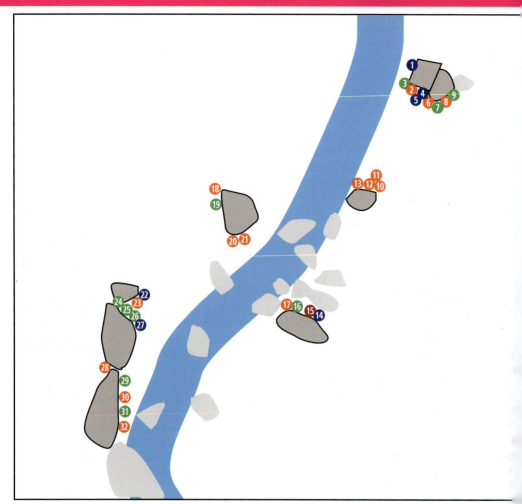

Full Throttle

84

# UPPER AREA - TUNNEL BOULDERS

Sole Slabs

he Upper Area can be accessed by hiking
ostream from the main area ~5 minutes or so.
the down and back is too much, then you can
ut down the hillside a couple hundred yards
efore you would ordinarily drop into the main
rea.

### Full Powder - V6
art at the northwest corner of the boulder
d traverse all the way around right on lip of
ulder finishing on Powder Edge.

### Powder Edge - V3
averse lip of boulder from left to right.

### Blockhead Mantle - V2
antle the southwest corner of boulder.

### Full Throttle - V7 ★★
is classic line starts standing as far back
the rail as possible in the little cave and
verses out to the face. At the end of the
, a committing move off of a bad left hand
mp/pinch at the lip takes you to better holds
vards the top. This line was supposedly
ginally done by going right hand to the crimp/
ch before gunning to the top rated at V8,
this seems unlikely, or at least not at that
de.

### Thrust - V7 ★
rt in the lowest pockets/edges on the
tom corner of the boulder and head up and
t to finish same as Full Throttle.

### ❻ Hot Rod - V0
This face problem faces the creek bed right next to the Cube Boulder. Start with right hand in pocket and climb face.

### ❼ Barely Legal - V3
Starts right hand sloper and left hand edge. Climbs out and up the arete.

### ❽ Street Legal - V1
Start three feet right of #7. Begin off the top of a small boulder with left hand on the arete and right hand on a blocky sloper.

### ❾ Le Coif - V5
Dead hang match on the big ledge behind the tree to start. Campus left to sloper and finish at the apex while avoiding the tree. Can start lower if you want to fight against dabbing even more.

### ❿ Sugar Daddy - V0
Sit start matched on edge in the overhang. Go straight up and right to top.

### ⓫ Sole Power - VB
Slab problem, arete off.

### ⓬ Sole Food - V0
Slab problem.

### ⓭ Sole Sister - VB
Climb smooth arete.

# LOS ANGELES COUNTY BOULDERING

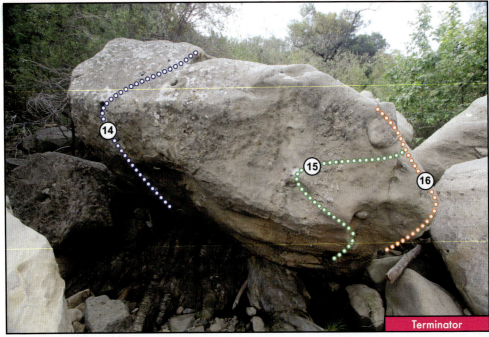
Terminator

**⓮ Terminator - V7 ★★★** ❑
This problem is a powerful beast with steep, long moves above a dicey landing. Start in head height pocket for the left hand and an undercling for the right. Go up and right through pockets to the top. A lower start which starts matched in the bottom hole goes at around V11.

**⓯ Procrastinator - V3 ★★** ❑
Stand start on sloper and cobble and climb up and right. During summer, when water is low, you can sit start on low flake/jug at V6.

**⓰ Pocketed Overhang - V2 ★** ❑
Sit start on low holds and go up overhanging prow then slightly right through pockets.

**⓱ T2 - V5** ❑
Start low on right side of prow. Climb up and left though pockets to jug.

**⓲ Pipe Dream - V2** ❑
Start matched on holds on the lip. Turn the lip and go up the face.

**⓳ Cobble in a Dish - V2** ❑
Starts in hole on knob and climbs up the arete.

**⓴ Lost In Space - V1** ❑
Start in hueco jug and go up to flat edge before turning lip.

**㉑ Man in the Moon - V2**
Start matched in hueco and head up through edges turning bulge.

**㉒ Blow - V6**
Starts hands matched on the far right sidepull undercling. Funky moves lead to the top.

**㉓ Street Legal - V2**
Start on the farthest left edge and traverse you way out the corner and up the short face to finish the same as Blow.

**㉔ The Sacking of Rome - V5 ★**
Starts sitting on large sidepull. Trends up and left on edges and pockets before a committing dyno. Watch your back if you miss the dyno.

**㉕ Kingpin - V4 ★**
Stand start at an edge and a slot. Traverse left to a seam before heading to the top. Ca also be done via a sit start extension which starts sitting in the cave at a grade harder.

**㉖ Druglord - V3 ★★**
Sit start on sloper. Head up through decent small edges to the same topout as Kingpin.

**㉗ Pablo Escobar - V7 ★★★**
Starts hands matched on undercling Work your way up technically powerful squeezes to the jug before a funky topout. Deceptively hard.

# UPPER AREA - TUNNEL BOULDERS

Pipe Dream

Druglord Boulder

87

# LOS ANGELES COUNTY BOULDERING

# UPPER AREA - TUNNEL BOULDERS

**Barracuda - V2**
Starts in the corridor. Climb steep face and right arete. Bad landing.

**Crawdaddy - V4**
Starts at big ledge. Climb up through crimps to a large shelf before going up and left through a seam to the top.

**Flydaddy - V2** ★
Climb up face off knobs to a large ramp before a big move up and left to top.

**Stuffed LeProhon - V3** ★
Start on small knobs and climb up to a match on a rail before continuing to top.

**Rock Lobster - V2** ★
Start on a big rounded edge going left to knob before throwing to a big jug.

Barracuda

Crawdaddy

89

# LOS ANGELES COUNTY BOULDERING

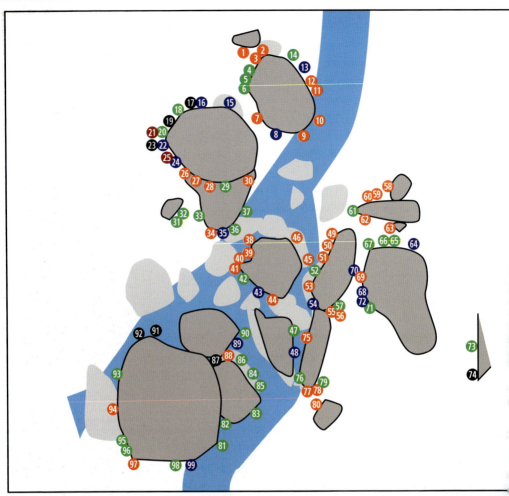

Cleft

# MAIN AREA - TUNNEL BOULDERS

Oasis

The Main Area is just south of the where the main trailhead drops into the canyon.

### Cleft Arete - V1
Start at head high holds and go up arete to top.

### Pit Arete - V2
Start on high left hand edge and a right hand pinch. Go up and left through small edges and sidepulls to top.

### Pit Problem - V0 ★
Start on sidepulls. Go up to large edge to a lip then.

### Oasis - V3 ★
Start on small edges and go up to small shelf and mantle.

### Bouldering for Dollars - V3 ★
Start left hand on sidepull and right on flat edge, head right and up though big reaches.

### Crawfish and Chips - V3
Start matched on small edges and finish on #5.

### Scoops - V0
Start matched on crimp rail and climb through scoops to top.

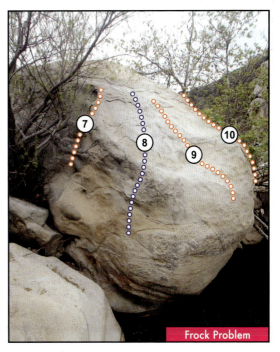

Frock Problem

91

# LOS ANGELES COUNTY BOULDERING

**8  Frock Problem - V6 ★ ★**
Start right hand in awkward pocket and left on slopey sidepull/edge. Go up to good edge and top out on tiny crimpers.

**9  Jumping for Mantles - V2**
Jump to slopers and mantle the slopey shelf.

**10  Jump Problem - V2**
Jump from boulder to a jug and top out. Don't fall!

**11  Oasis Seam - V1**
Head straight up the obvious seam.

**12  Oasis Arete - V1 ★**
Start just right of seam and follow the arete.

**13  A-Cups - V6 ★**
Start left side of boulder and traverse right though edges and perfectly rounded slopers to top.

**14  Midsummer's Daydream - V3 ★**
Start on underclings and go up through slopers to finish the same as A-Cups.

**15  Desperado - V6 ★ ★**
Start in huecos just to the right of the boulder. Traverse left and up through sidepulls and small edges to a rounded top out.

**16  Traverserado - V6 ★**
A fine extension of Desperado which starts at Over Lord and traverses left through some reachy/delicate moves to finish Desperado.

**17  Project**
This line has supposedly gone but there's some serious doubt associated with it. Start a few feet left of Over Lord and go up on small edges.

**18  Over Lord - V4 ★ ★ ★**
Start left hand on pinchy crimp sidepull, and right hand in hueco. Throw for big edge and top out with some technical footwork on small edges. Gets it's name from the "Thank God it Over, Lord" feeling once you top out.

**19  Project AKA The Great Undone**
Could be one of the most classic problems in the L.A. area! Climb small edges and slopers the apex of the boulder.

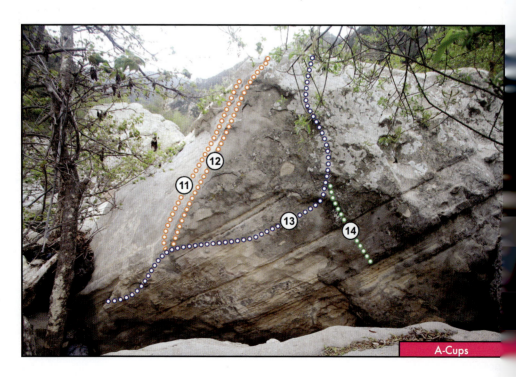

A-Cups

# MAIN AREA - TUNNEL BOULDERS

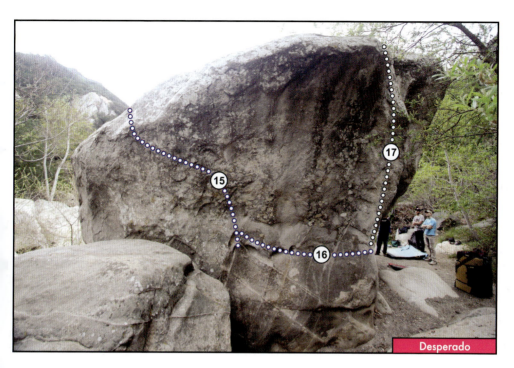

Desperado

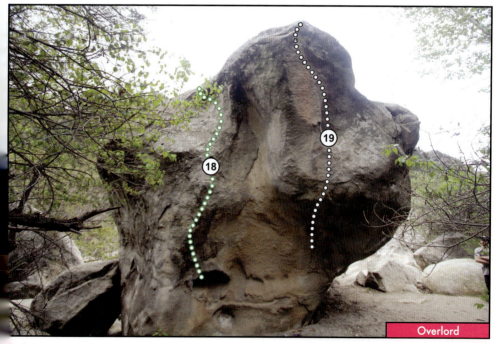

Overlord

# LOS ANGELES COUNTY BOULDERING

Avalon

**20  The Prow - V3** ★★★  ❑
Start right hand on open hand pinch and hop up to get left hand in pocket. Once established head up the seam/lieback.

**21  The Prow SDS - V12**  ❑
Sit start on friable edges to finish The Prow.

**22  Avalon - V8** ★★★  ❑
One of the classic hard problems in the area, done by Bill Leventhal back in 1989. Named after a beautiful model he worked with just before he put up the problem. Start hands spread out on edges just above head height and goes up through a crystal ball sloper, small edges and pinches to a committing top out.

**23  Project**  ❑
Links The Prow SDS into Avalon.

**24  Crocodile Rock - V6** ★★★
Start hands matched on huge shelf, go up and slightly left through some small edges to get to the lip. Arete on right is on for top out but don't exit into The Slide.

**25  Captain Hook - V9** ★★
Sit start with hands matched in hueco and head right through small edges. Throw to the shelf and finish via Crocodile Rock.

**26  The Slide - V1**
Start standing on large shelf and go up the scoop.

**27  Mantle - V0**
Start on large shelf. Climb straight up to a mantle ledge and top out.

# MAIN AREA - TUNNEL BOULDERS

# LOS ANGELES COUNTY BOULDERING

Malibu Lieback

**㉘ Malibu Lieback - V1 ★★**
Originally rated 5.8 but key footholds have broken at the start making it harder. Climb straight up crack. This is also the downclimb.

**㉙ Giant Step Unfolds - V3**
Start on small edges over a technical bulge to a thin face and straight up.

**㉚ DWP - V2 ★★**
Start in small pockets, head up and right through edges. A low start which starts on low edges and climbs through amazing slopers goes at ~V6.

**㉛ Spencer's Tree Problem - V3 ★**
Head straight up on flat edges to back of boulder up and left. Avoid feet on boulder to your left for the start.

**㉜ LeProhon Press - V3 ★**
Left hand on sidepull and right on small crimp. Reach for the lip and press it out.

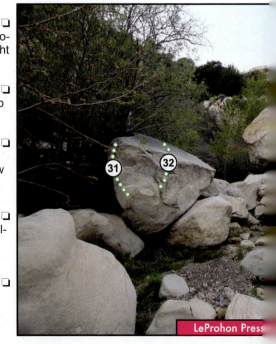

LeProhon Press

# MAIN AREA - TUNNEL BOULDERS

**33 Harder Than It Looks - V4** ★
Start on small edges at chest height and fire for the lip.

**34 Fraidy Cat - V2** ★
Start on high rail and climb up to shallow rail and left hand sidepull to the top.

**35 Yellow Belly - V6** ★
Starts on nasty sloper to the right of Fraidy Cat. Campus to rail before mantling huge sloping shelf.

**36 Arock Traverse - V3**
Start same as Fraidy Cat and traverse right along lip of boulder to high point.

**37 Fear Factor - V3**
Start on big shelf to underclings. Throw up and right before turning the lip.

**38 Small with Big Consequences - V2**
Start hands matched on incut rail. Reach out left over the water to shelf before mantling up and over.

**39 Test Tube - VB** ★ ★ ★
Stem your way up large scoop.

**40 X Arete Left - VB** ★
Climb left side of arete.

Party Slab

Test Tube

97

Bryan Hayes taking an evening stroll up X Problem. Photo: Sam Eaton

# LOS ANGELES COUNTY BOULDERING

X Problem

**㊶ X Arete Right - V2 ★ ★**
Climb the right side of arete.

**㊷ X Problem - V3 ★ ★ ★**
Climb up pockets and rails/ribs to a slopey top out.

**㊸ XXX - V7 ★ ★ ★**
Start left hand undercling and right hand on sidepull ~6 ft to the right of X Problem. Head up through slanting rails to rounded topout.

**㊹ Beluga Whale - V2 ★**
Start left hand on sidepull and right on a bad sloper. Make technical smears to a large shelf before you whale belly the mantle.

**㊺ The Cross Step - V2 ★ ★**
Climb up to and left through large slab scoop committing moves over the water to the arete.

**㊻ Slab - V1**
Many variations exist up the featured slab.

**㊼ The Natural - V7 ★ ★ ★**
Start hands matched on jug. Traverse left on perfect slopers to a big move and mantle into scoop.

**㊽ Seamless - V4**
Start on jugs and go straight up.

The Natural

## MAIN AREA - TUNNEL BOULDERS

ase Baron heading into the crux of Landing Not Included. Photo: Matthew Dooley

# LOS ANGELES COUNTY BOULDERING

Mutiny

Uprising

Flyboy

# MAIN AREA - TUNNEL BOULDERS

**49 Rebel Yell - V2**
Climb up from crimps past the flake.

**50 Revolt - V2**
Start matched on the lip and climb the face right of Rebel Yell.

**51 Power to the People - V2**
Start matched on the angled sloping rail and climb up and over.

**52 Mutiny - V3** ★
Start on slopey pinch and turn the lip.

**53 Underdog - V2**
Climb the arete.

**54 The Uprising - V6** ★
Start on underclings. Make a big move up and left to a sloper. Technical footwork will lead you to the good sidepull and beyond.

**55 The Lip Turn - V2**
Start matched on flat lip and mantle over.

**56 Flyboy - V2**
Start left hand at sidepull and right hand underling at chest height. Hard move to the sharp to finish on Lip Turn.

**57 Tension - V3**
Start standing with left hand on arete and right hand on crimp. Work your way up the arete.

**58 Small Fry - V2**
Climb up short blocky face.

**59 Warm-up - VB**
Climb featured face to jugs.

**60 Shit Crystal - V1**
Start left hand in shallow pocket. Stand on brown cobble and head upwards to jugs.

**61 Pinball - V5** ★ ★
Start down in pit and go up prow/arete using pockets and sidepulls. Best done when water is low.

**62 Monos - V2**
Start a few feet right of pinball in sidepulls. Climb up using small mono pockets.

**63 Spencer's Prow - V2**
This is the small V shaped block opposite El Diablo nestled up against a tree. Go up through sidepulls and slopers.

Pinball

# LOS ANGELES COUNTY BOULDERING

*El Diablo*

**64 Buck and Aron's Dirt Track - V6**
This line was apparently done as a mini solo. No known repeat ascents outside of the first ascentionists as of press time. Climbs up the brown streak.

**65 El Diablo - V5**
Originally a top rope but has been increasingly bouldered out. Climbs the right facing feature to a committing move to top. Gets its namesake from the climb looking like a demons face from the party slab.

**66 Beelzebub - V3** ★
Starts same a Diablo Overhang. Once at the big flake climb out and left to sidepulls to top.

**67 Diablo Overhang - V4** ★ ★
A classic of the area. Squat start low on sidepulls. Go up through decent holds to a jug before trending out left through gaston seam.

**68 Lycraverse - V8** ★ ★ ★
Starts left hand knob and right hand on big sidepull. Climb up and left using edges and slopers along the lip of boulder to finish same as Diablo Overhang. Harder if you're short.

**69 Lycra Boy - V2** ★
Stand start off boulder with hands matched on crescent hold and climb up brown stain.

**70 Lycra Linkup - V8**
Starts same as Lycraverse but exits about midway to finish Lycra Boy.

**71 Lycra Man - V3**
Mantle the big shelf.

**72 Lycrabolic - V8** ★
Same start as Lycraverse. Make a few difficult moves through slopers will take you to the top out via Lycra Man.

**73 Ode to the West Wind - V5**
Climb up edges to a seam and a dirty top-out. Watch out for poison oak on the descent.

**74 Project**
A climb which goes up the fin arete to hard compression seems somewhat feasible.

**75 Adam's Rib - VB**
Climbs slab along rusty streak.

**76 Balancing Act - V3**
Start on flake and mantle lip.

**77 Slap Happy Left - V2** ★
Sit start and climb through compression moves between the two aretes.

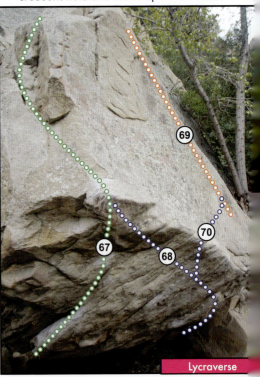

*Lycraverse*

# MAIN AREA - TUNNEL BOULDERS

Ode to the West Wind

**Slap Happy Right - V2 ★**
t start and climb through underclings to an sy topout.

**79 Slapshot - V3 ★**
Sit start based on arete and climb up and right through underclings to a funky lip turn.

Slapshot

# LOS ANGELES COUNTY BOULDERING

Apparatus

### 80  Sharkfin - V0
Several easy variations go up this face behind Slapshot.

### 81  Apparatus - V3 ★★
Start hands matched on sidepull and go straight up giant huecos to crux mantle. Maybe one day it won't be over water again.

### 82  Island Boulder Traverse - V3 ★
Original low start been lost due to the water. Start sitting on boulder with left hand on knob and right hand on slopey edge. Go up and right through pockets and sidepulls to a sloping mantle shelf.

### 83  Hungarian Traverse - V4 ★
Start back under the Island Boulder and traverse lip of boulder avoiding hand jams where the boulders meet. Finishes way over right.

### 84  Naked Man Overboard - V3
Starts sitting same as Teflon and traverses low and left through the roof to a big move out over the water to a hueco before topping out. To truly mimic the style of the first ascent, you need to get naked.

### 85  Under the Gun - V3
Climbs the steep huecos and undercling to a big throw to the lip.

### 86  Teflon - V4
Sit start matched on scoop, throw to sloper and mantle over.

### 87  Project
Climbs the tufa up the overhang to a scary ex over a pit.

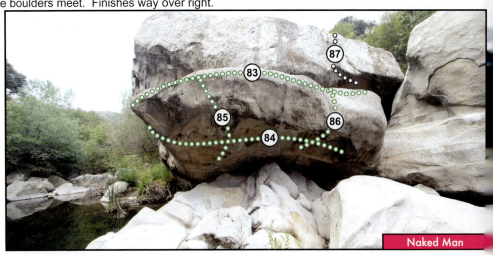

Naked Man

# MAIN AREA - TUNNEL BOULDERS

Landing Not Included

**Landing Not Required - V0** ★
art hands matched on sloper go up and left ough hueco.

**Landing Not Included - V7** ★ ★ ★
art hands matched on sloper and work your y up through big lockoffs on edges to the wn. As the name suggests, you'll have to ld a landing yourself if the landing has been shed away. Only wood pulled from the eam is allowed though.

**Intimidation - V3** ★ ★
nds matched on small sloper. Delicately ve to the hueco before following the arete op.

**Project**
imb up the obvious seam seems very feasi- Water landing has deterred many.

**Project**
nb out the prow from high pockets. Listed nother guide as Launch. General consen- is that this is still a project though.

Island Boulder Projects

# LOS ANGELES COUNTY BOULDERING

Islands in the Stream

Tête-à-Tête

# MAIN AREA - TUNNEL BOULDERS

5.10

### Islands in the Stream - V3 ★ ★
...assic overhanging problem. Go up edges/
...ckets, and sidepulls. Do not blow it as a fall
...ll end badly.

### Luckyman - V0 ★
...iginally started standing on boulder at big
...ck, climbing up through flakes and blocky
...ges. A lower start standing from a horizontal
...ture goes at ~V4.

### Better Than it Looks - V0 ★
...mb the right trending seam from a stand. A
... start to this checks in at around V4.

### Tête-à-Tête - V5 ★
...start on odd crimpers. Go up and left to a
... move to a sloper before heading up and
...r.

### 5.10 - V1
...mb the overhanging feature/arete.

### Recycle - V5
...rt left hand on small slopey edge and right
...pocket. Go straight up face to hueco/jug.

### Trash Compactor - V6
...ginally a toprope. Start at base of seam and
...up and right to hueco before mantling the

Trash Compactor

109

# LOS ANGELES COUNTY BOULDERING

Discarded Regard

The Picnic Area is located just a few minutes downstream of the Malibu Lieback Boulder and is approached via a trail that lead towards the road embankment behind Avalon. Follow this trail south until you see the picnic table. Discarded Regard and the face problems are located uphill from the table. The Recycler can be found by going over the picnic table, through a little rock passage, and then down into a pit of sorts.

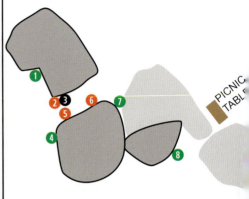

**❶ Discarded Regard - V5 ★ ★**
Climb up through small edges to huge jugs traversing right and up shallow dihedral to top

**❷ Off The Tree - V2**
Start off tree and climb up slab.

Off The Tree

# PICNIC AREA - TUNNEL BOULDERS

Face Problems

**Project**  ❏
...art in low envelope slots under overhang and ...mb into Off the Tree.

**Face #1 - V3**  ❏
...art right side of arete on small edges going ...t and up face/arete.

**Face #2 - V1**  ❏
...mb up through hollow flakes and edges.

**Face #3 - V1**  ❏
...art on huge flake and up through small edges ...op.

**Face #4 - V4 ★**  ❏
...mb up on small edges to slopers and awk-...rd top out.

**The Recycler - V4 ★ ★**  ❏
...mb up the tall face through edges and ...epulls to hidden jug on top.

**My Boy Bleau - V2**  ❏
...rt with left hand in undercling and right hand ...sidepull. Go up shallow trough to funky top

The Recycler

111

# HYPODERMIC AREA - TUNNEL BOULDERS

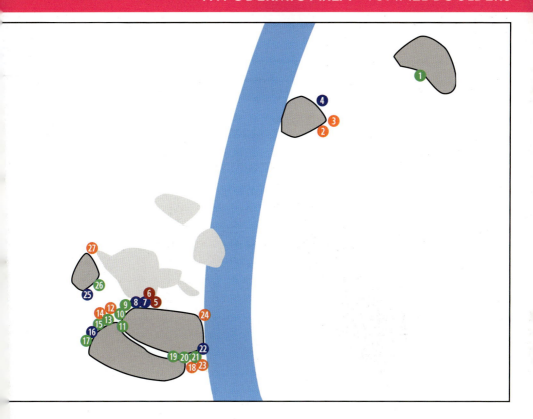

Neanderthal

# LOS ANGELES COUNTY BOULDERING

Samsquatch

Hypodermic

# HYPODERMIC AREA - TUNNEL BOULDERS

The Hypodermic Area is reached by walking downstream for ~5 minutes from the main area. Best way to approach is to head downstream from the Island Boulder via a faint path that leads you across the water and into a dry, cobbled creekbed. Follow the cobbled walkway for a ways until you see the Neanderthal Boulder on your left right off the path. The Bushwhack boulder is just past this on the right/stream side. The main Hypodermic boulders are located about another 100 yards past the Bushwhack boulder and are reached after a stream crossing.

**❶ Neanderthal - V3** ❏
Start hanging on the low triangle shaped bloc and traverse the lip until you reach the highest point.

**❷ Left of Arete - V1** ❏
From the hole in the middle of the face, climb straight up.

**❸ Baron Arete - V2 ★ ★** ❏
Climb the left side of the arete. The right side of the arete also goes and is ~V3.

**❹ Samsquatch - V7 ★ ★** ❏
Starting from underclings, climb up via tenuous moves past a small undercling and gastons.

**❺ No Honor Amongst Thieves - V9** ❏
Start on two low crimps. Move up and left to a angular crimp and a sidepull.

**❻ Roadkill Direct - V9** ❏
Start the same as No Honor Among Thieves. Climb up directly via a small crimp avoiding the arete.

**❼ Roadkill - V8** ❏
Start the same as No Honor Among Thieves. Traverse to the right on perfect crimps, finishing up the arete to a jug.

**❽ Save The Best for Last - V7 ★ ★ ★** ❏
Start same as Squirrel Head Roof. Climb into the overhang, and finish up the arete.

**❾ Squirrel Head Roof - V5 ★ ★** ❏
SS on pocketed pinch. Climb into the overhang and then exit early finishing up the face.

**❿ The Earlobe - V5 ★ ★** ❏
Start the same as Squirrel Head Roof. Go straight to a earlobe pinch and a big move to the lip before climbing the tall, but secure, top out.

**⓫ Junky - V4** ❏
Start left hand sidepull, right hand pocket. Climb up to a small edge on face and up to hidden hueco past sloper.

**⓬ Even My Girlfriend Does It - V0 ★** ❏
Stand start on finger pocket and hueco. Follow the series of huecos to the top. Boulder behind is off.

**⓭ Hypodermic - V2 ★ ★ ★** ❏
Start in large hueco and climb up via pockets and underclings to an incut rail. A fun mantle and positive holds lead to the top.

**⓮ Addiction - V0 ★ ★** ❏
Start the same as Hypodermic but traverse to the right on underclings to positive huecos.

**⓯ Feel the Rush - V4 ★ ★ ★** ❏
If the water level is low enough, start directly up the slab and climb up past a huge hueco and up through large undercling and small edges to the top. Can be traversed into if the water level is high. You definitely don't want to blow the top moves regardless.

**⓰ Gold Rush - V6 ★** ❏
Start on small rounded edges to oblong pocket to finish same as Addiction.

**⓱ Railed Out - V4** ❏
Climb up the rail features onto the upper slab.

Hypodermic

115

# LOS ANGELES COUNTY BOULDERING

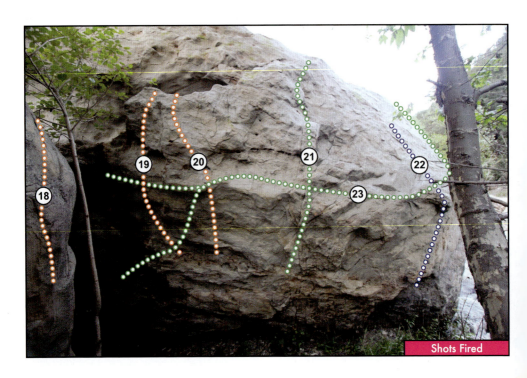

Shots Fired

Water Arete

# HYPODERMIC AREA - TUNNEL BOULDERS

Goldfinger

**Don't Move the Tree - V2** ❏
Climb either side of the arete on slopers.

**Unnamed - V1** ❏
Sit start on low left hand jug and right hand pocket. Climb straight up on good edges.

**Unnamed - V1** ❏
Sit start on low pockets. Climb straight up on pockets. Variations can be done going to the high pocket left or right hand at about the same grade.

**Unnamed - V1** ❏
Climb up edges from a low start to finish over the flake.

**Shot's Fired - V6 ★** ❏
Manage to pull yourself onto the wall with underclings before shooting to the jug shelf and mantling directly over.

㉓ **Squirrel Head Traverse - V3 ★** ❏
Start far left on big shelf. Traverse right via a variety of holds to a great finish around the corner on good sidepulls. Can also be started from a sit.

㉔ **Water Arete - V0 ★** ❏
Climb the arete on good edges. Best to wait until the water level is low enough to get your feet on at the beginning.

㉕ **Goldfinger - V6 ★ ★** ❏
Stand start with the left hand in the rust stained pocket and right hand on a poor incut feature. Hard moves between pockets leads to the top.

㉖ **Hieroglyphics - V4 ★ ★** ❏
Stand start. Work your way up small pockets style edges to the top.

㉗ **Unnamed - V0** ❏
Sit start right side of arete and climb to the top.

# LOS ANGELES COUNTY BOULDERING

Skidmarks

The Down by the River Area is located a couple hundred yards downstream of the Hypodermic area. To get there walk behind the Hypodermic boulder by Railed out and follow the jumbled ravine which parallels the stream. The boulders are right at the edge of the trees next to the stream

**❶ Unnamed - V1**
Starts matched in hueco. Climb up and right to sidepulls to top.

**❷ Skidmarks - V3 ★**
Sit start in pit and climb up face on edges.

**❸ Unnamed - V0**
Go straight up pockets and shallow huecos.

**❹ Red Spot - V2**
Start on solid edges at head height and head up to bigger edges through the red spot to top.

**❺ Toss for It - V4 ★**
Start on lowest crimps and bust a big move to a flat edge.

**❻ Approach Shoes - V7 ★★**
Same start as Toss For It, but at the flat edge traverse right to the arete.

**❼ Gato Cosmico - V9 ★★**
Start on low undercling crimps and climb up to join the finish of Approach Shoes.

**❽ Easy 1 - VB**

**❾ Easy 2 - VB**

**❿ Easy 3 - VB**

**⓫ River Arete - V1 ★**
SDS matched on slopers and work your way up arete.

**⓬ It Only Takes One Finger - V5 ★★**
Start on large sidepull flake. Make a big move left to a mono pocket and then up through shallow shelves and pockets to the top.

**⓭ Mantle - VB**

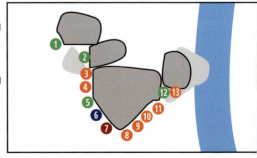

# DOWN BY THE RIVER - TUNNEL BOULDERS

Approach Shoes

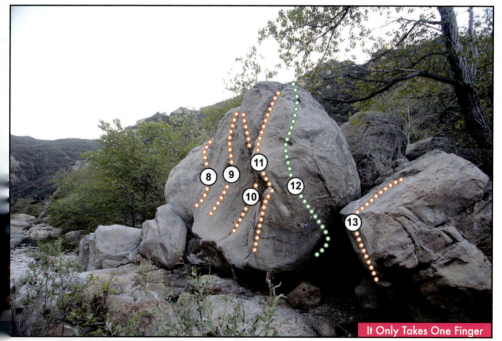

It Only Takes One Finger

# LOS ANGELES COUNTY BOULDERING

Something in the Bushes

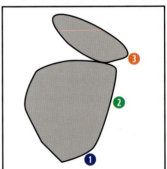

Leah is located a few minutes further downstream from the Down by the River boulders. This lone boulder is located right before a widening of the stream. The boulder is right on the edge of the water so if you hug pretty close to the stream you'll run right into it.

### ❶ Leah - V8 ★ ★
Starts sitting (don't try to cheat by stacking pads) matched on a limestone undercling. A hard move to get on is followed by big moves through slopers to top.

### ❷ There's Something in the Bushes - V5 ★
Start in sidepull and go up face past diagonal rail.

### ❸ Cougar Snacks - V2
Starts sitting at a good pod. Climb up and left along pockets to a tricky mantle encounter.

## SOMETHING IN THE BUSHES - TUNNEL BOULDERS

*Jesse Weiner taking advantage of evening temperatures on Leah. Photo: Devlin Gandy*

# MARTIAN'S LANDING

# LOS ANGELES COUNTY BOULDERING

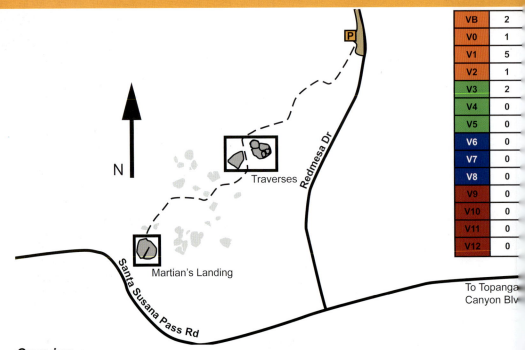

| VB | 2 |
|---|---|
| V0 | 1 |
| V1 | 5 |
| V2 | 1 |
| V3 | 2 |
| V4 | 0 |
| V5 | 0 |
| V6 | 0 |
| V7 | 0 |
| V8 | 0 |
| V9 | 0 |
| V10 | 0 |
| V11 | 0 |
| V12 | 0 |

## Overview
Martian's Landing is a collection of large boulders that offer the visitor one of the best cracks in Los Angeles and long traverses with relatively safe landings that's perfect for training. The rock is not as solid as the more well traveled rock to the east but for the climber seeking some solace or those wanting to explore, there are a handful of good problems scattered among the hillside. The crack amazing and unique, and as it lies low to the ground for most of it's length it's easy to work on the tougher spots.

## History
This area is often referred to as Garden Of The Gods, while climbers refer to it as Martian's Landi due to the namesake roof crack discovered around 1977 by Tony Yaniro. The namesake formatio is on the South end of the area, overlooking Santa Susana Pass road. The hill sides have lots of large boulders and lush, old growth oaks everywhere. The area is now called Garden of the Gods and it used to be part of the Spahn Ranch, a location where many movie westerns were filmed. We're talking Hop-a-long Cassidy, John Wayne, and Clayton Moore pardner. The Spahn Ranch also came to be known for being where Charles Manson & his followers resided. A spate of recen activity has resulted in the development of several long traverses and some other straightup problems. The rock might seem a bit gritty here compared to Stoney Point, but the rock is the same formation of sandstone. The grit found here is just indicative of the lack of traffic the area sees.

## Driving
Martian's Landing is accessed from Santa Susana Pass Road. SSPR is located ½ mile South of hwy 118, due West of Stoney Point by about ¾ of a mile. Turn West on Santa Susana Pass Roa and go ½ mile to Red Rock Mesa. Turn right and go to the top of the hill and park. Beyond this point are homes and parking is scarce.

## Approach
Access the boulders via a trail through the Garden Of The Gods. A short hike takes you to the fi boulders where the traverses are found. Two different trails head out from here, the one heading due West leads to a few of the other interesting boulders before curving left towards the split for tion that houses the Martian's Landing Crack.

# MARTIAN'S LANDING

Big Traverse

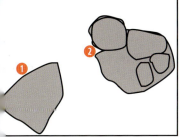

**❶ Big Traverse - V1 ★**
Traverse the largest boulder in either direction. The right to left is most popular, and many locals do laps back and forth.

**❷ Little Traverse - V0**
Traverses the steep features on the west face of the smaller traverse boulder. You'll cross two chimneys along its length. Most folks go left to right, ending where the rock turns a corner and goes into the hillside.

Little Traverse

125

# LOS ANGELES COUNTY BOULDERING

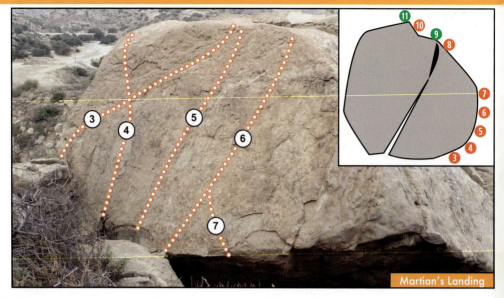

Martian's Landing

**❸ Descent Route - VB**
Climb the ramp that cuts across the face.

**❹ Jake's Face - V1**
Climb up on good rock, crossing the ramp and finishing directly.

**❺ Maggie's Face - V1**
Start in the center of the slab and go straight up on easier holds and join the ramp for its finish.

**❻ Bleau's Face - V1**
Step off the far right side of the launching pad and work up the slab above a rather large drop off.

**❼ Chossy Roof - V2**
Start in the left side of the alcove at a junky rail. Climb straight up using fragile edges.

**❽ Casual Route - VB**
A small foothold allows one to grasp the large holds above, friction up and right, finishing up blunt arete.

**❾ Martian's Landing Crack - V3 ★ ★ ★**
Climb the striking hand & finger crack through the roof to an awkward exit.

**❿ Junky Roof - V1**
Start 7 feet right of Martian's Landing Crack at good holds above the sloping overhang. Junky holds to turn the lip, better rock lies above.

**⓫ Old Skool Cool - V3**
Begin behind the small oak tree on the NW face. Steep crimps lead to a good pocket, a difficult step up leads to better edges and the top. Scary to commit over the lip!

Martian's Landing

# MARTIAN'S LANDING

m Eaton on Martian's Landing Crack. Photo: Bryan Hayes

# STONEY POINT

# LOS ANGELES COUNTY BOULDERING

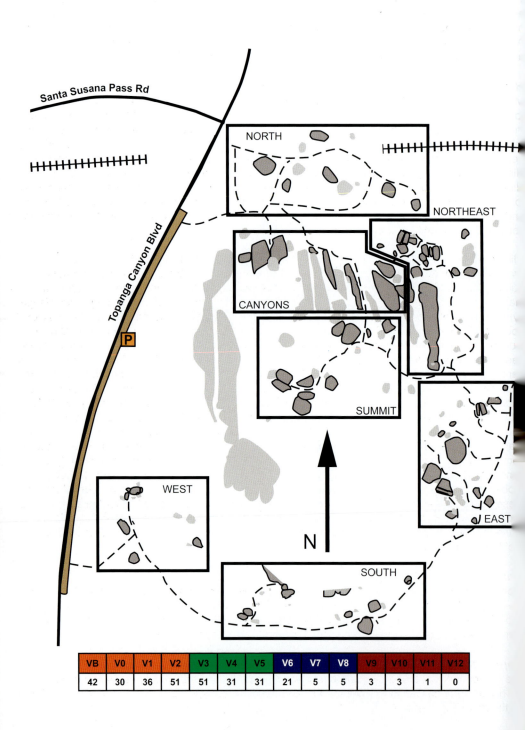

| VB | V0 | V1 | V2 | V3 | V4 | V5 | V6 | V7 | V8 | V9 | V10 | V11 | V12 |
|---|---|---|---|---|---|---|---|---|---|---|---|---|---|
| 42 | 30 | 36 | 51 | 51 | 31 | 31 | 21 | 5 | 5 | 3 | 3 | 1 | 0 |

# STONEY POINT

## Overview

The Stoney Point outcropping has dominated the north west corner of the San Fernando Valley for centuries. The formation is an Upper Cretaceous sandstone more then 65 million years old. With a view from the summit that takes in the whole valley, you could see how Native Americans and prehistoric man would be drawn to it. With its easily accessible summit and shady canyons, people have been enjoying Stoney Point for decades. This is documented by the numerous Native American artifacts that have been discovered in the area, as well as still existing grinding holes, and wagon tracks etched into the rock from years of constant travel.

## History

Members of the Sierra Club began to visit in the 1930's but few records were kept, as they tended to view it as strictly a "practice area". With Glen Dawson, Bob Kamps and TM Herbert being part of the early development . It was not until the 1950's that climbers began to visit more frequently and take the area more seriously as an excellent area for climbing. "Legends" of climbing cut their teeth here, Royal Robbins, Yvon Chouinard, John Bachar, John Long and too many others to mention climbed here. Stoney Point is a HUGE part of American rock climbing and has deep roots in the climbing world. The ease of access to both a freeway and a short approach from the parking, make for a terrific place that offers a quick visit or fun day of adventure. There are several good traverses and hundreds of boulder problems that cover the whole park. From the summit to the lower areas you can find something for every level of climber.

Climbers crawled all over SP for decades but it was never considered a bouldering area but a practice area for the big walls. A few classic boulder problems went up in the early days but the true classic from that era is Chouinard's Hole, a 60 year old boulder problem and a sandbag at that grade but a must do! Not until the 70's did climbers like John Bachar, John Long, Mike Waugh, Lynn Hill and John (Yabo) Yablonski helped develop SP into its own becoming more of a complete boulder field. Many new boulder problems started popping up and gems like Boot Flake, Umma Gumma, and Yabo Arete were born, becoming some of the life long classics at SP. Herb and Eve Laeger, Mike Jaffe, Jim Wilson along with Waugh were often working difficult boulder problems and harder eliminates that stymied many a visiting hardman. More development during the 1980's led to some of the more classic problems at Stoney Point. Yabo Arete, Kodas Corner, Sudden Impact and the seldom dome Arete-Me-Not are all products of this period. Activists from this group includ- ed Vaino & Toivo Kodas, Mike Guardino, Matt Oliphant, Bill Lebens, Bill Leventhal, Matt Dancy and others too numerous to name here. Around this time, a pair of strong guys was noticed to be tearing the place up! These two new upstarts would go on to bring a new level of difficult, highball, committing problems to the area which was always pretty stout to begin with! Even today, problems established by Jeff Johnson and Paul Anderson are well respected by modern climbers. New problems continue to be developed, although at a slower pace than in previous decades. Many of these new problems are difficult and show that Stoney Point still has more to offer the adventurous explorer. Many Stoney Point regulars go on Tuesday and Thursday afternoon/evenings. These gatherings tend to be spirited, lively affairs and many times you might encounter climbers doing problems by headlamp on a summer's evening.

## Driving

Stoney Point is located just ¾ mile south of the 118 freeway on Topanga Canyon Boulevard. If coming from the Ventura Freeway 101 you will go 9 miles north on Topanga Cyn Blvd through suburbia and mall heaven to the rustic environs of Chatsworth. Stoney Point has no parking lot so parking is found all along Topanga Cyn Blvd on the east side of the street..

## Approach

The approach to the bouldering is very simple with short walks to the boulders. Park at the base of the hill on Topanga Canyon Blvd to get to the south end of Stoney Point, and up at the top of the hill for the north end offerings

# LOS ANGELES COUNTY BOULDERING

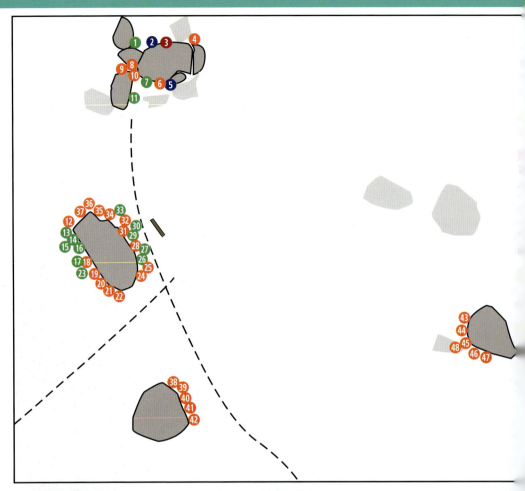

Crank Roof

# WEST - STONEY POINT

The Westside Boulders are located a stones throw from Topanga Canyon Blvd and is home to some serious classics. Park on the road near the Stoney Point sign and walk down the embankment. You can't miss them.

**1 Crank Roof - V1** ❏
Sit start climbing up and left to top.

**2 Cranking Queenie** ❏
These were once great problems and now it's just an abomination! No rating or stars because these problems have been hacked and fully desecrated from their original holds. Go in the cave and give your own grade and rating. There is a left exit or the bold John Bachar direct finish to top. Don't die.

**3 Crank Yanker - V9** ❏
Sit start at the base as for Crankin Queenie and head out left to Jam Crack.

**4 Jam Crack - VB** ★ ❏
Climb the crack.

Crankin Queenie

Jam Crack

133

# LOS ANGELES COUNTY BOULDERING

Say Goodnight

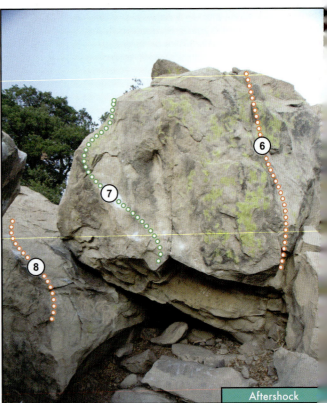

Aftershock

Pump Rock

# WEST - STONEY POINT

**⑤ Say Goodnight - V6 ★**
Start with left hand out on sharp sloper and right on small crimper. Go up and slightly left to top, right side of boulder is off.

**⑥ Unnamed - V0**
Climb the face. Don't fall!

**⑦ Aftershock - V5 ★ ★**
Start with right hand on good edge and jump up to large left leaning rail, match hands and continue up. This is a must do, John Yablonski classic.

**⑧ West Face - V2**
Climb up obvious left leaning arete of boulder.

**⑨ North Face Pump Rock - V0**
Climb straight up face to mantle top out.

**⑩ Pump Arete - V1**
Climb up slightly overhanging arete.

**⑪ Pump Rock Traverse - V3 ★**
Start with hands matched on top of left side of the boulder. Traverse right along the lip of the boulder all the way around to the north face and mantle out.

**⑫ West Arete - VB ★**
Start at big hold/ledge and go up through an envelope slot pocket, edges and side pulls.

**⑬ Nylon Boy - V4**
Start with hands on small rounded crimps and go straight up to a sidepull, and continue to the top.

**⑭ Bootflake - V3 ★ ★**
Start on flat edge around 5' off the ground, head up through side pull and up the boot to top left of boulder. It is one of the early classic boulder problems at Stoney. **Double Dyno (V5)** dynos from the start holds to the bootflake and then from the bootflake to the top..

**⑮ Bootflake Direct - V4 ★**
Same start as Bootflake but continue straight up to the top off of the boot.

**⑯ Gastoning - V5 ★ ★**
Same start as above but climb between Bootflake and Endo Boy on small sidepulls going straight to top.

**⑰ Endo Boy - V3 ★ ★**
Start a few feet right of Bootflake and go straight up through small edges, side pulls. Some technical footwork will help.

**⑱ Bob Kamps Face - V0 ★**
Climb up easy face.

**⑲ Short Story - V0 ★**
Funky high step leads to bomber sidepull and mantle finish.

Boulder 1 - West

# LOS ANGELES COUNTY BOULDERING

**㉠ Unnamed - VB**
Climb the face.

**㉑ Vivarian - VB**
Climb off ledge to top through decent holds.

**㉒ Descent Route - VB**
Easiest way down from the top.

**㉓ Boulder 1 Traverse - V4**
Traverse the whole boulder using the lowest holds and feet. Basically when you're at Stoney just ask Jan McCollum for beta because he has it wired.

**㉔ Southeast Corner - V2 ★**
Climb up the obvious corner.

**㉕ 10-40 - V2 ★**
Climb up crimps and past underclings.

**㉖ Three Pigs - V3 ★ ★ ★**
Head straight up the slots/pockets to edge at lip of boulder. This problem gets three stars based on its history as well as the climbing. Jon Doe chiseled this from atop his VW bus back in the 1970s when you could drive up to the boulders. Although a chiseled problem it has become a classic. Don't get it in your head that chiseling is okay here at Stoney though.

**㉗ The Real Yabo Mantle - V4**
Start just right of Three Pigs on small edges. Go up to an undercling and then mantle the shelf. Avoid the chiseled hold used for Vaino's Dyno in the center of the shelf and mantle on small edges and slopers.

**㉘ Vaino's Dyno - V4**
Dyno from opposing side pulls to chiseled hold on top center of shelf.

**㉙ Yabo Mantle - V4 ★ ★ ★**
Super classic and a must do! Start off opposing sidepulls climbing up through a small undercling pinch to rounded shelf and press out a mantle. Chiseled hold in shelf is off!

**㉚ Leaping Lizard - V4 ★**
Start same as Yabo Mantle and use left hand on shelf before dynoing to a small ledge up and right of the Yabo mantle shelf. **Static Lizard**, which goes at the same grade, climbs the same line as Leaping Lizard but avoids the dyno and opts for a static reach for the ledge.

**㉛ Vaino Reach - V3**
Start with hands matched on horizontal single digit edge. Trend left to sidepull and top out of the Leaping Lizard hold.

**㉜ Reach #1 - V4**
Same start as above but throw for big rail.

Boulder 1 - East

# WEST - STONEY POINT

**③ Reach #2 - V3**
Start with hands matched on horizontal single digit edge. Crank up to small edge above and then to top.

**④ Nose Arete - VB ★ ★**
Start hands matched on arete about head high and do some high stepping and pinching moves up to small shelf.

**㉟ Northwest Face - V2 ★**
Start on ledge and go up sidepull over bulge to edges and hueco finish.

**㊱ Dihedral Left - V2**
Climb up shallow dihedral finishing up and left.

**㊲ Dihedral Right - V3**
Go up and right to top out but watch the ledge cause you don't want to land on it.

Slant Rock

**Slant Rock Face Right - VB**
sy face problem.

**Slant Rock Face Center - VB**
sy face problem.

**Slant Rock Face Left - VB**
sy face problem.

**Slant Flake - V1**
start and climb seam up and left to top. ere is also a dyno from start holds straight o lip of boulder...very fun.

**Traverse - VB**
rt on the south end of the boulder and erse the lip.

**㊸ Unnamed - V0**
Climb the left face.

**㊹ Unnamed - V1**
Climb the face just left of the prow.

**㊺ Unnamed - V2**
Climb up obvious prow from a sit start.

**㊻ Unnamed - V1**
Climb the face just right of the prow.

**㊼ Unnamed - V0**
Climb the face past a big hole.

**㊽ Unnamed - V3**
Traverse around the boulder in either direction.

# LOS ANGELES COUNTY BOULDERING

Hillside

*A rattler enjoying it's rabbit lunch a stones throw from Boulder 1. Be careful out there. Photo: Matthew Dooley*

# WEST - STONEY POINT

*McKenna Murphy high up on Bootflake. Photo: Spencer Josif*

# LOS ANGELES COUNTY BOULDERING

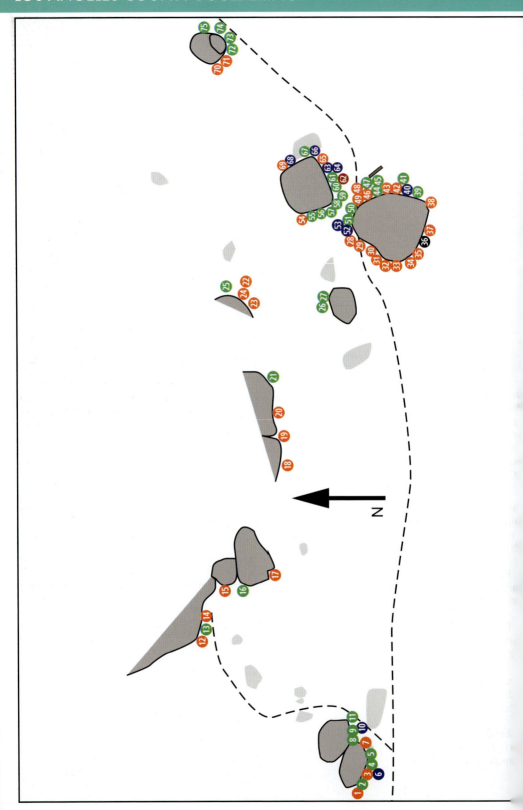

140

# SOUTH - STONEY POINT

Pile Ups

The Southside Boulders can be found by following the trail due east from the gate along Topanga Canyon Blvd. First cluster of boulders you'll come to is the Pile Ups cluster. The Amphitheatre climbs are up behind these boulders and the Turlock boulders are about 50 yards further east

**Pile Ups Traverse - V2** ★ ★

Traverse the lip of boulder from left to right. Going from right to left goes at same grade. Rumor has it that John Bachar has the record up there and back over 10 times.

**Pile Driver - V3** ★

Start hands matched on the pointy jug and climb up through small crimps to top.

**Pile Lieback - V2**

Start on decent edges and go up through sidepulls to top of boulder.

**Gomer Pile - V3**

Undercling start and go up and right through sidepulls and crimpers.

**Sledgehammer - V4**

Start on decent edges and go up through sidepulls to top of boulder.

**❻ Low and Behold - V8**

Starts hands matched on left side edge of boulder. Traverses right through the middle of the boulder on funky edges and underclings.

**❼ Pile Ups Mantle - V2**

Mantle the lip.

**❽ Scary Face - V4**

Great line but suspect rock makes for few ascents.

**❾ Ghetto Bird - V5** ★

Start on opposing sidepulls/flakes. Climb direct, up crimps and slopers to good holds at the apex of the boulder.

**❿ Angel Wings - V6**

Start on a decent left hand sidepull and a right hand crimp. Traverse right through a small edge to a good hold at the corner before a big move leads to top.

**⓫ Unknown - V4**

Sit start on corner of boulder.

There's a ton of variations on the face to the right of #11 as well, including a few mantles. No names for these but they're pretty fun.

# LOS ANGELES COUNTY BOULDERING

Amphitheatre

**⑫ Mike's Up Problem - V0**
Climb straight up the left side of the wall to a gritty finish.

**⑬ Amphitheatre Seam - V3 ★**
Climb straight up seam through thin pockets to dirty top out.

**⑭ Amphitheatre Traverse - V2 ★**
Traverse the length of the wall in either direction. Both ways go at the same grade.

**⑮ Easy Face - VB**
Straight up the middle of the face.

**⑯ Thaw Dyno - V4**
Start on good edges and dyno to black patina edges. Easy moves from there get you to the top. Watch the landing.

**⑰ Black Roof - V0 ★**
Climb up wide slot crack in roof.

Black Roof

# SOUTH - STONEY POINT

Sierra Club Bluff Left

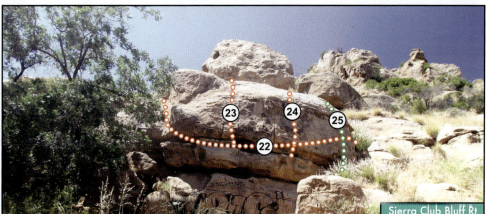

Sierra Club Bluff Rt

**Juan Carlo Problem - V1**  ❏
pposedly climbs out the dirty roof and up
e.

**Unnamed - V0** ★  ❏
mb the left most crack.

**Unnamed - VB**  ❏
mb the right crack.

**Lance's Problem - V5**  ❏
start the blunt arete to slopey top out.

**Sierra Traverse - V5**  ❏
verse right to left going up and through the
i dihedral section to finish.

**Sierra Face - VB** ★ ★  ❏
mb up obvious face starting hands matched
head high slopey jug.

**Unnamed - V1**  ❏
epulls and crimps lead to tricky mantle.

㉕ **Unnamed - V3** ★  ❏
Climb the face at the upper end of the bluff.

㉖ **Unnamed - V4**  ❏
From a large blocky feature traverse right on
slopers to finish around the corner on the slab.

㉗ **Unnamed - V5**  ❏
Climb the short face to a sloping mantle.

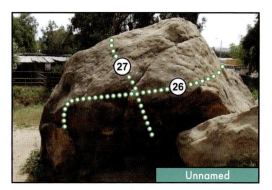

Unnamed

143

# LOS ANGELES COUNTY BOULDERING

Turlock

**㉘ The Corner - V2 ★ ★**
Start left hand on rounded undercling and right hand in pocket. Climb up to rounded lip and out crack.

**㉙ Silent Running - VB ★**
Start at sidepull pockets going up through seam to crack, following crack to top.

**㉚ The Flake - VB ★**
Climb up right angling flake to a rounded topout.

**㉛ Turlock Face - V2**
Start on small edges and shallow scoops. Climb up slab.

**㉜ Downclimb - VB**
This is the easiest way down from the top  Use huge buckets to downclimb.  Also a good climb for beginners.

**㉝ The Bulge - V0 ★**
Start hands matched in huge hueco, traverse left then up to shallow three finger pocket, en at downclimb. **Bulge Direct** is the same start but go up and right to slabby top out.

**㉞ Potholes Face #1 - V0 ★**
Start same as the Bulge but trend up and rig through a large hueco to top.

**㉟ Untold Story - V1**
Start on decent edges and climb up through large hueco to finish same as above.

**㊱ Point Blank**
Old school problem that has broken over the years...Basically undone as is.

**㊲ Potholes Face #2 - V0 ★**
Many variations on this tall face, which are excellent warm ups.

# SOUTH - STONEY POINT

Turlock

**Southeast Arete - VB**
Climb the obvious arete on either side to a tall finish.

**Ramada - V3**
Start on slopey dish and climb up edges and pockets to huge jug finish.

**The Real Crystal Ball Mantle - V6 ★**
Climb out of giant rounded undercling through small edges and mantle sloping shelf.

**Slime - V3 ★**
Many variations but basic start is hands in undercling and going up and slightly left through edges to the big ledge at half height.

**Pliers - V2 ★**
Start with left hand on face high edge and right hand crimpy pocket climbing up through obvious edges to rounded finish at the ledge.

**Hoof and Mouth - V2 ★ ★**
Start with hands in undercling or jump into the hueco climbing up and left to rail.

**44 Nose Dive - V5 ★**
Same start as Hoof and Mouth but go straight up through small edges on a blunt arete to top. Very heady!

**45 Over the Hoof - V3 ★**
Start with hands matched on good edge going up and left over hoof and mouth hole along small edges to a good rail.

**46 Turlock Prow - V2 ★**
Same start as Over The Hoof, but continue straight up prow using technical footwork and a cool head.

**47 Bob Kamps Mantle - V3 ★**
Mantle small rounded edge on face about head high. Right sidepull at start is on, press out a left hand mantle to a rounded shelf. All other holds are off!

**48 North Face - VB ★**
Climb straight up obvious face.

**49 North Face Flake - VB ★**
Climb up face to right facing flake and up to the top.

# LOS ANGELES COUNTY BOULDERING

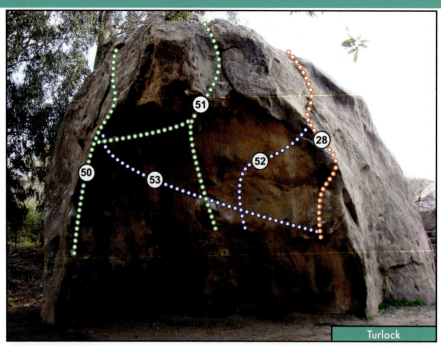

Turlock

**50 Yabo Roof - V3 ★ ★ ★**
Start with left hand on small edge left of arete and right on decent sidepull. Climb up arching arete through flakes to funky lip turn.

**51 Crowd Pleaser - V4 ★ ★ ★**
Jump up to crystal ball jug and go straight up to top. Originally started at Yabo Roof and traversed right to finish but done direct more commonly now. When you're on it you'll see why they call it crowd pleaser!

**52 Waugh Problem - V6**
Jump up with left hand on slopey shelf and right hand in jug, climb up through mono pocket to seam exiting out right on Corner Problem

**53 Anderson/Johnson Traverse - V7**
Start on the Corner and traverse up and left finishing on Yabo Roof.

John Hu floating through Yabo Roof. Photo: Matthew Dooley

# SOUTH - STONEY POINT

m Eaton bearing down on Ed's Direct. Photo: Spencer Josif

# LOS ANGELES COUNTY BOULDERING

**54 B1 Corner - V2**
Begin on sidepulls and go up and left, on good holds.

**55 Hog Tied - V3**
Climb up obvious jugs to a committing finish.

**56 Master of Reality - V5 ★ ★**
Old school classic! Stem your way up to good edges, finishing on a proud exit. **Masters Chamber** is a variation that tops out on Expansion Chamber starting on Master of Reality.

**57 Expansion Chamber - V5 ★ ★**
Another Old School must do! Left hand on big sidepull and right on shallow dish. Climb up to small crimps using desperate smears to a funky top out.

**58 The Ear - V4 ★**
Start hands on edges at the bottom of large hueco and go straight to top up through undercling and small edges.

**59 Inside Out - V4 ★**
Same start as The Ear, awkward movement going slightly right on mostly good holds gains the top.

B1 Boulder

**60 ELP - V5 ★**
Start left hand in small shallow pocket and right hand in larger pocket. Climb up to small ledge and then slightly left through edges to top. A right variation goes off of small ledge to sidepull flake up and right is V5.

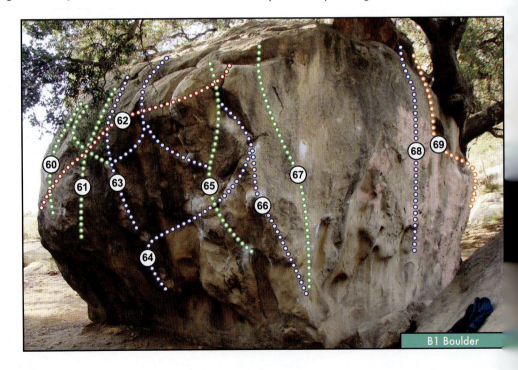

B1 Boulder

148

# SOUTH - STONEY POINT

**61 Pink Floyd - V4** ★
Jump start to undercling hold with left hand and right on Apesma sidepull. Crank to slopey sidepulls and mantle top out. Another Mike Waugh variation uses left hand starting in ELP right hand hold and jump up grabbing undercling with right hand going up to mantle finish.

**62 Ed's Traverse - V10** ★
Follows a high line starting on The Ear and traversing up and right finishing on the top out of The Crack.

**63 Apesma** ★ ★ ★
There are three separate Apesma lines here - Apesma Left, Center and Right. All three are stand starts out of the same two finger pocket. **Apesma Left (V5)**, starts left hand in the two finger pocket going up to the main Apesma hold and then left finishing on the Pink Floyd mantle. **Apesma Center (V8)** starts with your right hand in the two finger pocket and going to through main Apesma hold to a small crimp just above the bulge, topping out directly. **Apesma Right (V6)** is the same start as Center, but moving right off main Apesma hold to shallow sidepulls and top out.

**64 Titty Fuck - V6** ★ ★ ★
Squat start with hands matched on round undercling hold (the tit) and climb up to the two finger pocket, trending out right finishing on The Crack. **Ed's Direct (V10)** is the same start but finishing out Apesma center. **Titsma (V9)** is another variation off the tit which finishes on Apesma.

**65 The Crack - V3** ★ ★ ★
Start with hands matched on obvious sidepull, climb up through odd shaped holds slightly right to a rounded top out. **Crack Direct (V3)** is same start but straight up using only the crack. **Cracksma (V6)** starts the same and goes up and left, finishing on the sidepulls of Apesma right.

**66 The AG Pinch - V6** ★ ★
Same start as the crack but reach out right hand to a pinch and climb up good holds to a rounded topout. Sit start is V8.

**67 Flying Circus - V4** ★
Left hand on large sidepull at head high and right hand on small sidepull crimp going up through slot shaped edge and a final move takes you to the top.

**68 Neal Kaptain's Horror - V8** ★
Starts left hand on sidepull crimp and right hand in shallow two finger pocket. Powerful moves lead to monos and edges to the top. Recent breakages have made this way harder.

**69 Two Scoops - V2** ★ ★
Start on the corner of the boulder going left through the scoops and up to obvious jug. A couple variations exist, **Scoopless (V3)** goes from the same start, straight up above the pinch climbing the edge of the formation to top.

**70 Unnamed - V2**
Sidepull and shallow pocket takes you up through crimps to the top.

**71 Unnamed - V2**
Climb through big pocket to slopey top.

**72 Unnamed - V3**
Climb short slabby face.

**73 Unnamed - V3**
Climb up through cap to top.

**74 Unnamed - V4**
Crimpy moves lead to top.

**75 Unnamed - V4**
Mantle to short slab.

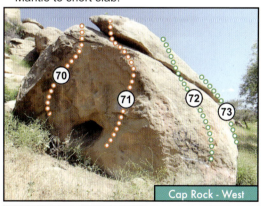

Cap Rock - West

Cap Rock - East

149

# LOS ANGELES COUNTY BOULDERING

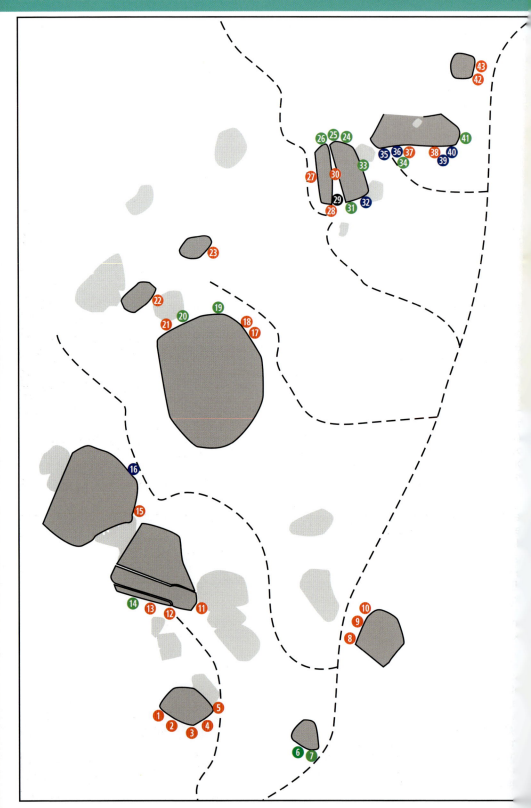

# EAST - STONEY POINT

Stock Rock

Stock Rock Slabs

The Eastside Boulders can be found by following the trail due east from the Southside boulders. Some of the boulders are obvious from the trail while others can be reached via small trails leading uphill.

**Easy Money - VB**
Start below a large hueco on the right side of the south face. Follow knobs and flakes to a good finish.

**Black Monday - V2**
Climb the thin face.

**Black Friday - V2**
Climb the narrow band, using small sloping flakes and edges, this will test your footwork!

**Bull Market - V3** ★
This one climbs the face without using the arete to the right. The finishing moves are a bit heady.

**Corner the Market - V3** ★ ★
Climb the arete on its left side. The start of this is the crux if you don't use the slab below, if you do the route is V0. Right side of the arete goes at about the same grade.

❻ **Lion's Head #1 - V3**
This one is literally on the trail. Pretty simple too. Just mantle.

❼ **Lion's Head #2 - V4** ★
Harder Mantle.

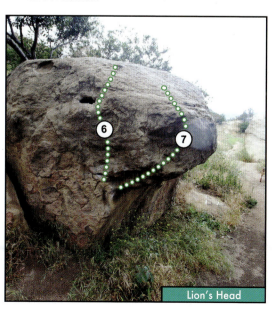

Lion's Head

151

# LOS ANGELES COUNTY BOULDERING

Pyramid

**8 Unnamed - VB**
Climb over bulge at the eastern end of the pyramid to top.

**9 Unnamed - VB**
Climb up and left using seam in the middle of the face.

**10 Unnamed - VB**
Climb the right side of the face.

**11 Meatgrinder Mantle - V0**
Mantle slopey shelf to slab.

**12 Flake - VB ★**
Climb flake.

**13 Face - V2**
Climb the face just left of the flake.

**14 Sugar Pops - V3**
Climb the face from the obvious start.

Slab Rock

# EAST - STONEY POINT

*Spencer Josif finishing off Sudden Impact. Photo: Jenna Isenberg*

# LOS ANGELES COUNTY BOULDERING

Sudden Impact

**15** **Pie Slice - V1** ★
Climb the hand & fist crack.

**16** **Sudden Impact- V6** ★ ★
Climb piton hold pockets in the seam to top. Originally top roped but has been bouldered out over the decades. Bad landing but super classic line, a must do

**17** **Bold During - V1**
Old problem. Rock is Junk.

**18** **Borealis - V0**
Climb the face above a horrendous landing.

**19** **Spiral Traverse - V3** ★ ★
Classic traverse going left to right. Can be done either way but most people start down left.

**20** **Spiral Direct - V3**
Start on small edges and up through undercling to top.

**21** **Spiral Direct II - VB**
Climb up face off of rail.

Spiral Traverse

# EAST - STONEY POINT

Chouinard's Slab

Slap

**Chouinard's Friction Problem - VB** ★ ❏
imb short slab opposite Spiral Traverse.

**Slap - V1** ❏
imb the lowball face.

**Darkside of the Moon - V5** ★ ❏
art sitting and climb right and up through thin
opey edges, arete can be used.

㉕ **Vaino Problem - V5** ★ ❏
Climb the right arete.

㉖ **Johnson Arete - V4** ★ ❏
Climb the arete. Considerably easier since
some kook chiseled an unnecessary hold.

㉗ **Valdez - V1** ❏
Climb up the easy face.

Johnson Arete

155

*Jeff Johnson on his namesake arete. Photo: Damian Gebert*

# EAST - STONEY POINT

Split Rock

**Arete Skeleton - V2**
art off boulder with hands in large hueco, mb up face and arete.

**Project**
mb up face via giant moves...one of the last at undone problems at Stoney.

**Chimney - VB ★**
mb the chimney.

**③ Split Decision - V3 ★ ★**
Face moves lead to a crack with a committing last move.... Another top rope thats been bouldered so much we had to put it in.

**④ Johnson Problem - V6 ★ ★ ★**
Probably one of the greatest problems at Stoney Point and a true must do line. Start left hand on large rounded side pull and right hand on small right facing crimp. Climb up to huge jug and over bulge to top.

n unfortunate finding. Leave the glue at home for your Arts and Crafts projects you kooks!

# LOS ANGELES COUNTY BOULDERING

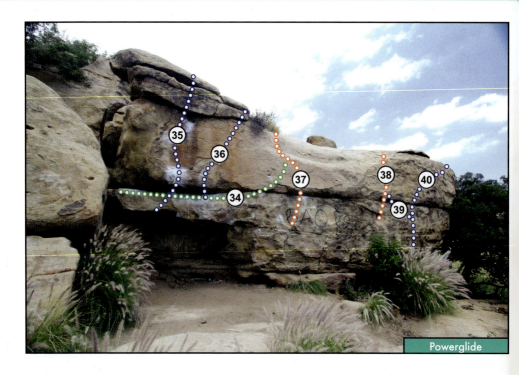

Powerglide

**③ Super Natural - V5 ★**
Start hands matched on good holds climbing up and right to small rounded edges to slabby top/finish.

**④ Eat Out More Often - V5 ★ ★**
Traverse horizontal seam left to right.

**⑤ Snot Here aka Powerglide - V6 ★ ★ ★**
Start hands matched on good rail and then up to envelope slot holds climbing through thin crimper to bomber hold that leads to easy top out. Originally done as a dyno from the envelopes slops skipping the crimp.

**⑥ Lynn Hill Problem - V7 ★**
Starts on thin crimpers to the right of envelope slot holds. Desperate undercling/gaston moves up face through decent edges to top.

**⑦ Standard Route - V2 ★ ★**
Hands start matched on good hold in horizontal crack going up to small crimps and topping out through triangle notch.

**⑧ Renaissance Man - V2 ★**
Start hands matched on good hold at head high, kind of a hop step off boulder to get feet on. Then climb up and off slopey shelf to top..

**⑨ Mosaic Thump**
Squat start and climb up to the horizontal cra before traversing left to finish the same as Re naissance Man. Recent breakages have ma this unrepeated in it's current form.

**⑩ Tree Route**
Same as for Mosaic Thump but finish directly

**⑪ Bachar Dyno**
       **aka Dynamic Duo - V5 ★ ★**
This problem is found on the east face of the formation facing the trail. Start on good face hold and sidepull dynoing off of two finger pocket and sloper to rounded top.

*Just past the Powerglide boulder on the left hand side of the trail is a boulder with the below lines.*

**⑫ Trailside #1 - VB**
Climb the left side of the face.

**⑬ Trailside #2 - VB**
Climb the right side of the face.

*Past the trailside boulder, there's another cluster of boulders dubbed the Land of Gian with easy lines scattered around. While not detailed in this guide it may be worth checki out if you've done everything else.*

# EAST - STONEY POINT

# LOS ANGELES COUNTY BOULDERING

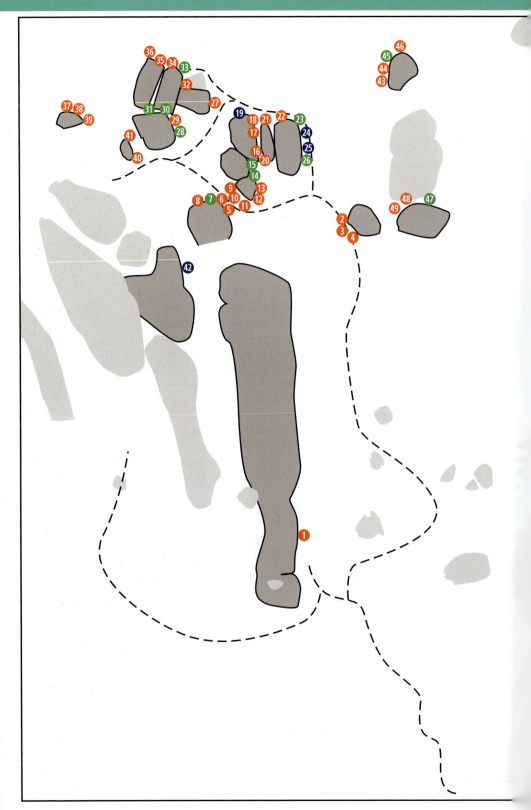

# NORTHEAST - STONEY POINT

Potholes Traverse

The Northeast Boulders are best approached by parking at the North end of Stoney along Topanga Canyon before the light at Santa Susana Pass and hiking in along the North side of the area. That being said, these boulders can also easily be reached from the south via a trail leading up and away from Johnson Arete.

**❶ Potholes Traverse - V2** ★ ★
Traverse goes both ways but mostly starts from right to left. Decent edges and technical feet gets you across this favorite of Bob Kamps so pay your respect to the plaque that has been placed there in his honor and climb on holds that legends of the past frequently visited.

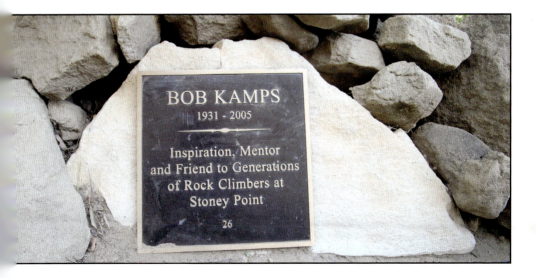

# LOS ANGELES COUNTY BOULDERING

Broken Boulder

**② Unnamed - V2**
Climb up and right along the lip of the boulder to the apex.

**❸ Unnamed - V1**
Climb up to the apex of the boulder starting on a large undercling.

**❹ Unnamed - VB**
Easy climb using pockets.

Broken Boulder

# NORTHEAST - STONEY POINT

Scrambled Eggs

**The Crack - V2**
traight up crack.

**The Birdhole - V1**
limb up seam through large hueco.

**Scrambled Eggs Traverse - V3 ★ ★**
raverse from right to left to finish the same as
he Birdhole

**Shorty Shea - V0**
limb the tall face from start of the traverse.

**Unnamed - VB**
limb face.

**Unnamed - VB**
limb the middle of the face a few feet left of
e arete.

**Unnamed - VB ★**
mb the left side of the arete.

**Unnamed - V0**
mb thin flakes on face.

Unnamed

163

# LOS ANGELES COUNTY BOULDERING

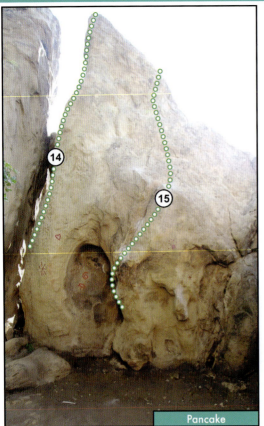

Pancake

### ⓭ Flake to Nowhere - V2
Climb the lieback flake exit up and left on edges to the top. Old school climb, doesn't get done much due to loose rock.

### ⓮ Kodiak Corner - V3
Climb right leaning arete. Sometimes this one is dirty.

### ⓯ Pancake - V4 ★
From a sit, climb the crack and mantle.

### ⓰ Ozone Factor - V1
Climb face, tread carefully on loose flakes..

### ⓱ Critter Crack - V0 ★ ★
Classic crack.

### ⓲ Mantlelobotomy - V1 ★
Start hands matched on slopey undercling and climb up through small edges to the mantle.

### ⓳ The Font - V6 ★ ★
Start on sidepulls in the skull shaped pod and climb up through pockets to a heinous mantle on slopers. This shouldn't need to be said, but the chiseled hold in the sloper to the right is off and should not be not used.

### ⓴ Easy Face - VB
Climb face in the corridor.

Mantlelobotomy

# NORTHEAST - STONEY POINT

The Font

**Blocky - V1**
Climb blocky prow going up and right.

**Hedgeclipper - V2** ★ ★
Junky start gets you up to shallow dish continuing up to spooky top out.

**Alien - V5**
Start on sidepulls and small edges to some technical moves along the arcto to top.

**㉔ Fritz Face - V6** ★ ★
Start hands matched on undercling and climb up tiny edges to slopey top out.

**㉕ Microscope - V6** ★
Start low on a sidepull and go up right to thin rail with tiny edges and then to top.

**㉖ Scorpion - V5** ★
Same start as microscope but climb straight up on small edges.

Fritz Face

# LOS ANGELES COUNTY BOULDERING

Puggie

Guar Scar

**㉗ Puggie - V0**
Climb through the bulge via horizontal edges.

**㉘ Eightball - V3 ★ ★**
Start on left side of face going up and right to rail. Continue up to eightball ho past decent edges to top.

**㉙ Earthquake Face - V3 ★ ★**
Start hands matched on good hold and go straight up large sloping edges to tl top. Kind of spooky but fairly solid.

**㉚ Incubus - V4 ★**
This problem starts down in the little notch using small edges to seam.

**㉛ Guar Scar - V3 ★ ★ ★**
Classic line! This gem follows the thir seam inside the chimney. It starts on right hand edge in dish going up throu the seam to top.

**㉜ Mazzi Corner - V2 ★**
Climb left side of arete.

# NORTHEAST - STONEY POINT

Kodas Corner

**Kodas Corner - V3 ★ ★ ★**  ❏
Climb right side of arete using the flake/edge to the right to gain the arete midway up before an exciting mantch. Using the arete only has been done and is V6. A classic.

**Unnamed - V2**  ❏
Climb arete to the right of Kodas Corner but to the left of the chimney.

**Unnamed - V2**  ❏
Climb arete to the right of the chimney.

**Billy Bob Arete - V2**  ❏
Climb the rounded arete

**The Hood**  ❏
Climb the face in any of several variations. Holds have broken and this seems to be significantly harder now.

**Down in the Hood - V1**  ❏
Start same as above but finish on arete.

**Arete - V0**  ❏
Climb the smooth arete next to the Hood following mostly big holds.

Down in the Hood

167

# LOS ANGELES COUNTY BOULDERING

Left/Right

**40 Left Problem - VB**
Climb left side of boulder.

**41 Right Problem - VB**
Climb right side of boulder.

**42 Plunger - V6**
Climb up and left with a committing finish on the rounded arete/prow.

Plunger

# NORTHEAST - STONEY POINT

**Unnamed - V1**
Climb the tricky arete, harder than it looks

**Unnamed - V2**
Traverse the face along a sloping rail to the spout of the The Hood.

**The Radulator - V3 ★**
Climb up to the sloping shelf and make difficult moves to gain the top of the boulder.

**Unnamed - V2**
Climb the West face of the boulder following a shallow vertical scoop/pocket to edges trending up and left to the top.

**East Canyon Traverse - V3 ★**
Traverse the north face of the canyon starting low and left and work up and right to a tricky move around the arete to finish up the final slab.

**Blunt Arete - V1**
Climb the blunt arete using small edges and toe balance.

**Matt's Face - V2 ★**
Climb the slab on the NW face using smears and boot magic.

Radulator

East Canyon Trav

169

# LOS ANGELES COUNTY BOULDERING

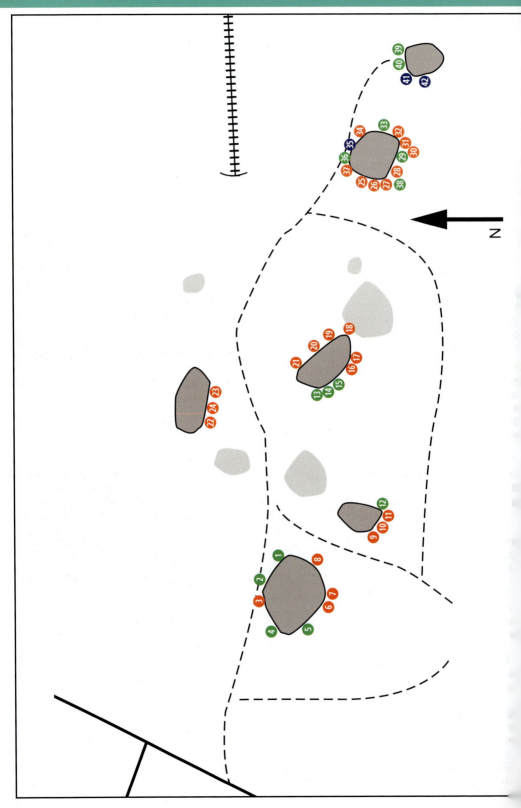

# NORTH - STONEY POINT

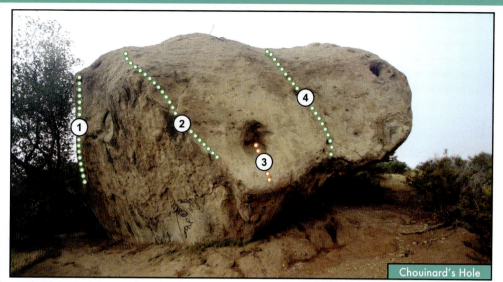

Chouinard's Hole

The North Boulders are (surprise) located along the North boundary of Stoney point along the tracks. These boulders are best approached by parking just south of the light [at] Santa Susana Pass.

**Buckets to Bag Dad - V3** ★
[O]n the NE face, just right of a small oak tree. [St]art on good edges to hueco, then use edges [up] and left so you can move up slab to top. [Th]e nearby Oak tree can obscure some of the [ho]lds on occasion.

**Arete Me Not - V5** ★ ★ ★
[Cl]imb the left leaning arete that is immediately [left] of Chouinard's Hole. Techy moves on slop[py] crimps lead to a rewarding juggy finish.

**Chouinard's Hole - V2** ★ ★
[Cli]mb into hole. Harder than it looks. Most folks [b]ack in from the right side. Topping out is a [bit] heady but not too bad.

**Half Gram - V3** ★
[Sta]rt on undercling 8' right of Chouinard's Hole [bel]ow a basketball size hueco. Gain this and [ju]mp up pocketed seam to the top.

**Bush Doctor - V3**
[Cli]mb up crusty edges through giant hueco, [pu]shing up and right to top...scary finish!

**Pocket Face - V0**
[Cli]mb up through large pockets to easier [clim]bing.

**Jingus - V2**
[Pl]us face through shallow pockets to round[ed t]op out.

❽ **Northwest Face - VB**
Several variations ascend the slab.

❾ **Southwest Corner - V1**
Climb the arete just left of the obvious crack.

❿ **Split Crack - V0**
Climb the crack from a low start.

⓫ **West Face - V2**
Climb the face 5 feet right of the crack.

⓬ **South Face Overhang**
Climb the overhanging arete, holds have broken making this harder than it used to be.

Halfway Humpback

171

# LOS ANGELES COUNTY BOULDERING

Slanderland

**13 Trouble Told - V4 ★**
Climb up into the shallow scoop and proceed straight up.

**14 Bad Press - V3**
Climb the center of the face past edges and slopers to the top.

**15 Slanderland - V4 ★**
Climb up the right, center of the face past edges to a rail and top out.

**16 Sleazy Tabloid - V0**

**17 Reggae Route - V1**
On the far right side of the face, begin at a big, rail/jug & climb up sloping edges and pockets and more crimpy edges to the top.

**18 Holy Shit - V1 ★**
Climb up shallow huecos, passing a carved hold down low, that lead to sloping holds to the top.

**19 5.10 Face - V1 ★**
Difficult moves get you standing in the large pocket 10' off the ground, delicate moves lead to the top.

**20 5.9 Slab - V1**
Gain the slab starting on the right, work up and right, passing 2 bolts, towards the arete to the top.

**21 Daily Circuit - V1**
Climb the NW end of the boulder past a small overhang below a prominent hueco and either finish up the arete of the 5.9 slab, or continue up the ramp to the right.

Slanderland

# NORTH - STONEY POINT

Slanderland II

**Route Rustlin' - V1 ★**
mb the left side of the face passing a shal-
 hueco up high.

**Yard The Tool - V1 ★**
mb the center of the face up to prominent
ckets.

**㉔ Alice in Slanderland - V1**
Traverse the face of the boulder from right to left.

WWWWHHHHHYYYYYY?????!!!!??!?!?!?!?!?

# LOS ANGELES COUNTY BOULDERING

Carousel

**㉕ West Face - V0 ★**
Start just right of the tree. Climb up and right along the crack.

**㉖ Face and Crack - V0**
Same start as above but exit directly instead following the crack out right.

Carousel

# NORTH - STONEY POINT

**㉗ Unnamed - V0**
Sit start on undercling. Climb up through pockets to the crack and finish same as West Face.

**㉘ Center Route - V0**
Climb up on slopers.

**㉙ Mantle Problem - V5 ★**
Slap out left to a decent edge in the big pod of Center Route before pulling through to a pocket and a mantle.

**㉚ Face - V2**
Climb up via sidepulls and an undercling.

**㉛ Southwest Corner - V0**
Climb the face using edges and sloping pockets to an easier topout.

**㉜ Carousel Edge - V1**
Climb the arete/rib of the formation above the path.

**㉝ Carousel Face - V4**
Begin at and ear shaped hueco, climb above using small crimps and edges to the top.

**㉞ Rollercoaster - V2 ★**
Climb up and left past a pocket to a ledge. mantle the ledge prior to committing to the tall thin face.

**㉟ Night Train - V8**
Climbs just to the right of Rollercoaster through the large undercling and past worsening holds to the apex of the boulder.

**㊱ North Face - V5 ★**
Climb up the skull shaped pocket before moving out right to finish on the blunt arete.

**㊲ Arete - V2 ★**
Climb the blunt arete on the either side. Left side goes at V2. Right side at V1.

**㊳ Carousel Traverse - V5**
Traverse the entire Carousel Boulder in a clockwise direction. Could tell you where to start but since you have to go all the way around does it really matter?

Carousel

175

# LOS ANGELES COUNTY BOULDERING

**㊴ Largonaut - V4 ★★**
Climb the NE arete of the boulder beginning on top of a boulder on the left. Start hands matched on decent reachable edge making technical moves to top. Starting off the ground is the lower start going at V8. It starts with right hand on small sidepull edge and left pinching outside edge of boulder following original line to top.

**㊵ Router Bit - V5 ★★**
Climb the center of the N face using manufactured horizontal slots and edges to the top.

**㊶ Yabo Arete - V6 ★★★**
Super classic at Stoney Point! This amazing route tackles the NW arete of the boulder. Begin with a difficult compression move to get started, powerful moves lead up edges and pockets to the finishing arete moves.

**㊷ Cleared for Takeoff - V6**
This seldom done line goes up the W face of the boulder using distant edges and crimps. Tough moves up high keep most suitors at bay.

Block Head

Block Head

# NORTH - STONEY POINT

*Largo running a lap on Yabo Arete. Photo: Bob Gaines*

# LOS ANGELES COUNTY BOULDERING

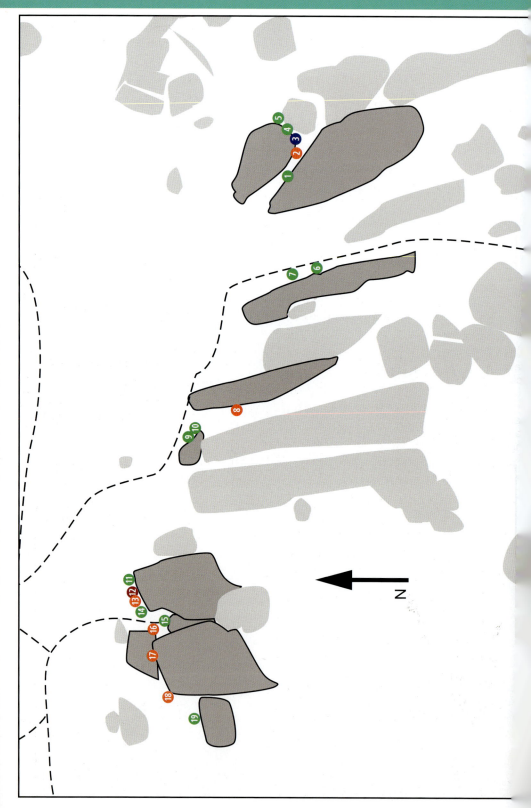

# CANYONS - STONEY POINT

Mozart's

The Canyons are all located along the North side of the Stoney Point Formation. Easiest approach is by parking at the North end of the parking along Topanga Canyon.

**Mozart's Traverse - VB ★**
Traverse the wall starting on either side. Most locals start on the left.

**Quickstep - V2 ★**
Start with sidepulls on the left and pockets in the seam on the right. Go up to a big jug topping straight out.

❸ **Seam Stealer - V6 ★**
Straight up pocketed seam to thin top out. Holds out left are off.

❹ **Hand Crack - V3**
Go up to jugs and climb flaring hand crack.

❺ **Sandlow Problem - V5**
Starts on right side with bouldery moves to gain the rail. Finishes all the way right passing the crack.

Quickstep

# LOS ANGELES COUNTY BOULDERING

Sculpture's Traverse

**6 Sculpture's Traverse - V3 ★ ★**
Starts on right side with bouldery moves to gain the rail. Finishes all the way left passing the namesake crack.

**7 Sculpture's Eliminate - V5**
Climb the face to finish on the rail of Sculpture's Traverse.

**8 Maggie's Traverse - V1 ★ ★**
Start on left traverse all the way up and right. Top out or reverse to the start.

Maggie's Traverse

# CANYONS - STONEY POINT

**9 Texas Flake - V0**
Climb the face of the boulder via a balancy mantle over a poor landing.

**10 Texas Flake Arete - V1**
Climb the overhanging face using large semi-loose patina flakes up and out to the final arete to the top.

Hot Tuna

**Hot Tuna - V5 ★★★**
Start left hand on side pull, right hand on shallow dish. Traverse left to right. Finishing on the lopey jug.

**Cold Sushi - V10 ★**
This problem starts deep in a seam past the second hueco. Start on full-pad crimp to start right hand on, with the left matched on a smaller crimp to the left. Make difficult moves requiring an insane amount of tension out the roof before continuing to the top out and left.

**Seam - V2**
Start on large rail go up through seam to big edge. Traverse off left.

**Bachar Mantle - V5 ★**
Start hands matched on shallow dish. Go up through jugs to shelf and mantle. Stand up on shelf and hop off.

**Mickey Mouse - V5 ★★**
Start low in the crack. Head up the crack before exiting up and left over the bulge on jugs.

Mickey Mouse

181

# LOS ANGELES COUNTY BOULDERING

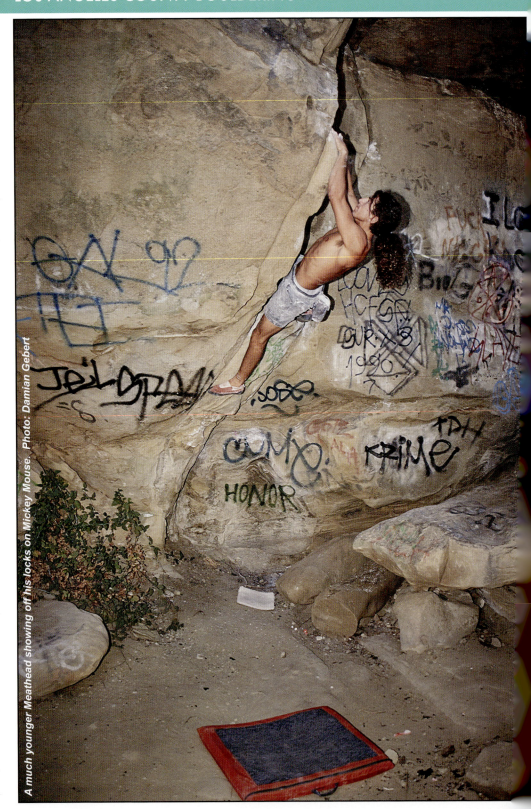

A much younger Meathead showing off his locks on Mickey Mouse. Photo: Damian Gebert

# CANYONS - STONEY POINT

Undercling

**6  Arete - V1**
Climb the arete from a sit start.

**7  Undercling Traverse - V0**
Climb the crack up then left. Down climb or top out.

**18  Crack Hand Traverse - V1**
Start at underclings go up through jugs to crack traverse off right.

**19  Reardon's Problem - V5 ★**
Start off boulder at large hueco. Go up through small pocket and edges to top.

Reardon's

183

# LOS ANGELES COUNTY BOULDERING

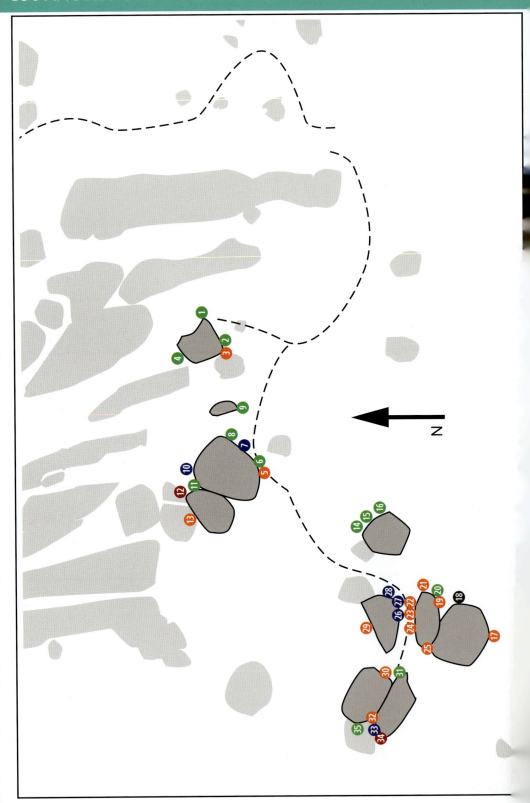

184

# SUMMIT - STONEY POINT

Flash Me

Depending on where you're coming from The Summit Boulders are best approached via the Sculptures crack Canyon (if approaching from the north) or up the trail to the southern end of the Potholes traverse (If approaching from the south).

**Flash Me - V3 ★ ★**
Start sitting on boulder with hands on the obvious good holds. Traverse left on lip of boulder all the way around and up arete toping out on high point of boulder.

**Face Problem - V5**
Originally done as a stand but there is a sit start that's a grade harder. Start on small edges at chest height and climb through hueco to top.

**Sticky Fingers - V2**
Start hands jammed, kick feet up and climb out crack.

**④ Johnson Mantle - V6**
Difficult mantle with an awkward lip turn.

**⑤ Ummagumma Crack - VB ★**
Climb up the obvious crack.

**⑥ Hein Flake - V3 ★**
Climb the rounded edge of flake just to the right of Ummagumma Crack past a pocket to top.

**⑦ Guarglaphone - V6 ★ ★**
Cheatstone start for this one. Start with hands on tiny rounded crimpers going up and right to killer pocket. There you encounter an intimidating lip turn/mantle.

**⑧ Ummagumma - V4 ★ ★**
Super classic! Start hands in large hueco firing for small pocket. From here the original line exits right, but you can finish directly or to the left as well. Each is a great finish. Left exit is V6 and the direct is V5.

Ummagumma

185

*The Verm himself highstepping his way to the top of Ummagumma. Photo: Damian Gebert*

# LOS ANGELES COUNTY BOULDERING

**⑨ The Hawk - V3**
Climb the small prow located behind you when looking at Ummagumma.

**⑩ Old Man and the Point - V7 ★ ★**
Located just around the corner to the right from Ummagumma. Starts left hand on shallow divot style hold and right hand on single digit sidepull. Climb up tiny edges and ok slopers through mono pocket to top.

**⑪ Roof Crack - V4**
Start at beginning of cave and climb roof crack to the other side.

**⑫ Fighting with Alligators - V11 ★**
Sit start and climb up and right through the prow and then along lip of boulder using slopers/edges along the lip to help you along this burly traverse. Pull over at the jug midway in the face. A direct finish which tops out directly from the first lip match goes at ~V10.

**⑬ Rodeo Style - V2**
Direct start below the finishing jug of Fighting with Alligators.

Old Man

Alligators

# SUMMIT - STONEY POINT

Rodeo Style

**Unnamed - V3**
Climbs the right side of the face along the rounded prow. Exciting landing.

**Unnamed - V3**
Climbs the center of the face past underclings over a spooky landing.

**16 Unnamed - V3**
Climbs the left arete.

Hillside

# LOS ANGELES COUNTY BOULDERING

Skull Rock

**17 Flakes - V0** ❏
Climb up via good flakes.

**18 Project** ❏
The tall arete seems like it should go. If not it's a freaking shame.

**19 Unnamed - VB** ❏
Easy face.

**20 Left Arete - V3** ❏
Climb the left arete via sidepulls.

**21 Right Arete - V2** ❏
Climb the arete from the pocket.

**22 Mommy's Boy Left - VB ★** ❏
Easy left side of the face.

**23 Mommy's Boy Center - VB ★** ❏
Climb the center of the face on small edges.

**24 Mommy's Boy Right - V2 ★** ❏
Can you guess? Climb the right side of the face. Starts a few feet left of the undercut.

**25 Jaws - V1** ❏
Climb the highball face starting in the corridor.

Mommy's Arete

# SUMMIT - STONEY POINT

Mommy's Boys

**Yabo Dyno - V8 ★ ★**
art low on decent edges before climbing out
ht to a dyno from a sidepull and small edge
rounded hold. Very deceiving problem, looks
sy but one of the hardest dynos at Stoney.

**㉗ Potato Chip - V7 ★**
Climb decent to small edges to top.

**㉘ Don't Touch the Banana - V6 ★**
Start hands matched on huge jug, climb
straight up to top.

Yabo Dyno

# LOS ANGELES COUNTY BOULDERING

Pocket Traverse

**㉙ Pocket Traverse - V2** ★
Traverse the wall from left to right. Crux is at the end so keep something in the tank.

**㉚ Face - V2**
Climb up obvious face to top.

**㉛ Offwidth - V4**
Climb the very obvious offiwidth crack.

Offwidth

# SUMMIT - STONEY POINT

Cry Uncle

**Jam Crack - V1**
Climb the obvious had crack.

**Cry Uncle - V6 ★**
Difficult moves past an undercling get you to the top.

**㉞ Two Worlds Collide - V9**
Climb the blank rounded arete from a sit start.

**㉟ Niles Reardon Traverse - V2**
Double boulder traverse. Start out left and traverse to the Face on the other side of the corridor.

The Valley ....

# LOS ANGELES COUNTY BOULDERING

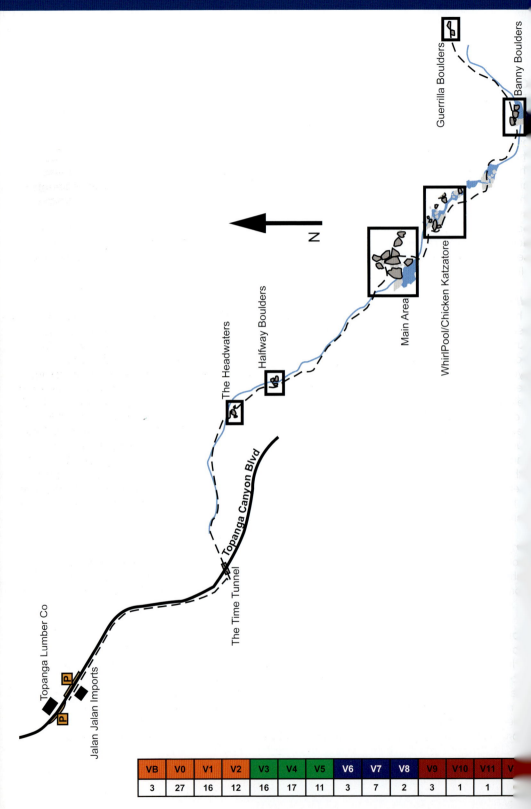

# PURPLE STONES

### Overview
The Purple Stones is a year round, intermediate to advanced boulder field nestled down in the creek bed of Topanga Canyon on near perfect water polished sandstone. Most boulders have a purple tone to them hence the name purple stones or as they called it back in the day, the twin poles, which dates back to the 60's as a swimming hole and a nice place to party. They called it the twin poles because from the creek bed you could see the two telephone poles on the road that hung out over the canyon and marked the main area. Long before any climbers the naked hippies frolicked and sun bathed nude down in the canyon. Lying around the creek bed enjoying the lush canyon and on some kind of psychedelic probably. Rumor has it that the Manson family used to frequent the swimming hole as well. It was a very popular area to hang out when you could park anywhere along the canyon. It is more of a popular bouldering area than a swimming hole nowadays though you will still get the occasional group swimming around down there. Afternoon sessions are usually best because morning can be a little damp from morning dew but still can be climbable, windy days are good because of the low humidity.

### History
The Purple stones were visited by Joe Mckeown and other climbers in the early 1970's. We can assume they did some of the easier lines, but they kept no records. The main development occurred when Banny Root discovered the area and started bouldering down there with David Katz, Bob Gaines, and Robert Carrere. Later they brought the likes of John Long, Mike Lechlinski and Lynn Hill. In the mid 1980's Bill Leventhal, Matt Oilphant, Mark Fekkes and Bill Lebens began to frequent the area, developing new problems and adding some new top ropes which even today, are seldom repeated. A long period of quiescence resulted when the old parking place was closed and the old trail became overgrown by brush and poison oak turning the area into jumanji. In 2008, a new spate of development began when Banny Root & Bill Leventhal revisited the area via the Time Tunnel and discovered the Headwaters area. Many new climbers began visiting with Dimitriuc Fritz and Spencer Church developing some fine new problems along with Devlin Gandy, Matt Dooley & Chan Gia who put up many hard problems as well. New problems have continued to be discovered and the adventurous type might be able to find more. Most of the bouldering is not for the faint of heart since most of the boulders are very tall with bad or wet landings. So be wise when climbing here and know your limits.

### Driving
From the 101 freeway head south on Topanga Canyon Blvd for 8.5 miles to a dirt pullout on your right/west side of Topanga canyon Blvd and there's parking across the street as well. From Pacific Coast Highway 1 head north on Topanga Canyon Blvd for 3.5 miles to the dirt parking area, this will be on your left/west side.

### Approach
From the parking area head south on Topanga Canyon Blvd for 0.3 miles or about a 5 to 7 minute walk to the second guardrail on your right/west side. It can be a bit sketchy in spots because the shoulder gets about a foot wide and traffic can be scary. About ¾'s of the way along the second guardrail you'll see a faint trail on the west side of the rail. This will take you around to, "the time tunnel", a 7' wide cement pipe that goes under the road to the creek bed. You'll make a right at the creek bed and head down stream for a few minutes until you come upon the Headwaters boulder. From the Headwaters boulders continue down stream for 7 to 10 minutes to the main area.

# LOS ANGELES COUNTY BOULDERING

Thimble

**❶ The Bowling Ball Problem - V0**
Climb up the slab past the bowling ball shaped hold.

**❷ Headwaters Arete - V4 ★**
Start at the base of the round arete and head up on cobbles and edges.

**❸ The Thimble of The Santa Monicas - V5 ★ ★ ★**
Start standing on opposing sidepulls at chest height. Delicate moves between slick cobbles and edges leads to an exhilarating move to the lip. For full style points, and to mimic the method of the FA, the ramp of the dihedral is off.

**❹ Headwaters Ramp - V0**
Head straight up the small, shallow dihedral

**❺ Headwaters Traverse - V4**
Start sitting on the left arete and traverse across on cobbles to finish on Headwaters Ramp.

**❻ Mantle - V0**
Mantle the bulge to the right of the top of Headwaters Ramp.

Headwaters Boulder

# HEADWATERS - PURPLE STONES

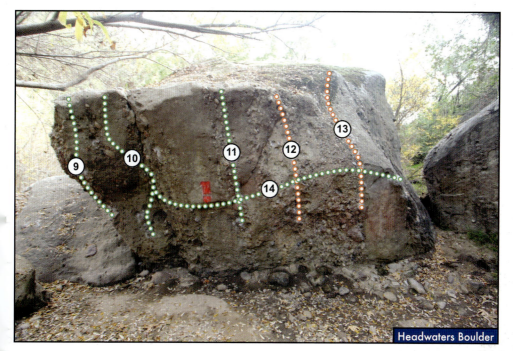

**Gaslight Lantern - V5**
Start same as Maple Canyon Arete and trend left on edges/pockets before mantling over.

**Maple Canyon Arete - V3** ★
Start the arete on opposing pockets. Big first move with the left hand to a crimp leads to easier compression climbing through cobbles and pockets.

**The Inbetweener - V4**
Same start as Maple Canyon arete but climb up the prow between Maple Canyon Arete and The Seam.

**The Seam - V4** ★
Start at a left hand pocket and a cobble for the right. Climb up along the seam feature via a series of sidepulls and pinches.

**The Centerpiece - V5** ★
Start at a large cobble. Climb up through an undercling and some flat edges before hitting a high left gaston to gain the lip.

**When the Levee Breaks - V2** ★
Start at funky cobbles and pockets. Climb through a hollow jug and dishes before a big move to the lip.

**⓬ Number Nine - V0**
Stand start at the vertical pinch and climb up along the cobblestone border.

**⓮ Soapstone Traverse - V5** ★
Start at the far right side of the boulder on the arete. Traverse the length of the boulder, topping out the same as The Seam. An extension of this traverse can also be done into Maple Canyon Arete. **Don't Drop The Soapstone Traverse** does the same line but left to right and goes at about the same grade.

**⓯ Backside Warmup - V0**
Starting with thin moves climb up and right through holes to finish up and left of the alcove.

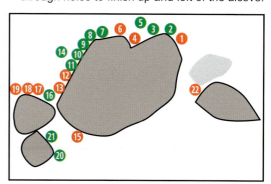

199

# LOS ANGELES COUNTY BOULDERING

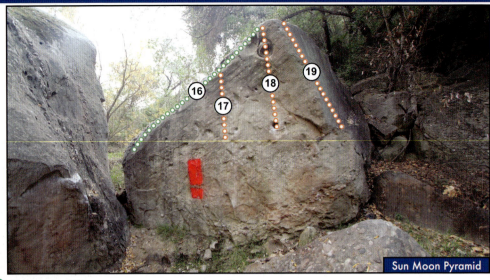

Sun Moon Pyramid

**16 Traverse - V3**
Start in dimples on left side of the face and traverse up the lip to the apex of the boulder.

**17 Talibanny - V1**
Start on small edges going up through sidepulls and pockets to the top.

**18 Illuminati - V1** ★ ★
Start in a hole at eye level. Climb straight up through Sun Moon feature.

**19 Corner Pocket - V0**
Start hands matched on shelf and go up through mono pocket to rounded top out.

**20 Purple Haze Traverse - V4**
Starts sitting at the left arete of the boulder. Traverse the lip of the to the topout of Spencer's Roof.

**21 Spencer's Roof - V4**
Starts underneath the boulder on two pockets. Climb up and to the left, being careful to avoid the dab. Be careful and make sure you're not setting up in a patch of poison oak before trying this.

**22 Garrett's Pit Problem - V2**
Climbs the short face in the pit between the two boulders on the trail.

Spencer's Roof

# HEADWATERS - PURPLE STONES

Andrew Rothner on The Thimble of the Santa Monicas  Photo: Matthew Dooley

# LOS ANGELES COUNTY BOULDERING

Halfway Boulder

Halfway Boulder

The Halfway Boulders are located about 5 minutes downstream of the Headwaters area. The stream cuts directly through this concentration of boulders.

### ❶ Unnamed - V5
Sit start matched on a sloping shelf. Work your way up the double arete face to the top via pockets.

### ❷ Purple People Eater - V9 ★
Sit start matched on the same sloping shelf as #1. Left hand to a shallow dish before making big tenuous moves out to the right arete and then back to the left to hug your way to the top.

### ❸ Harmonica Lewinsky - V5 ★
Starts on a right hand sidepull and left hand on the arete. A few moves put you on a perfectly horizontal rail before the mantle. Blowing the mantle is not an option, as a fall from the top, even with spotters, will likely end with you in the water strewn over rocks. A lower start which starts on the undercling has also been done at around V7 if you don't mind a tight squeeze.

# HALFWAY BOULDERS - PURPLE STONES

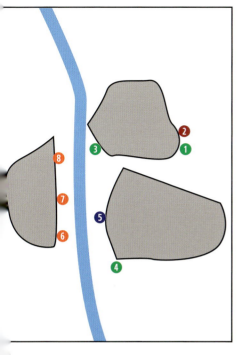

Halfway Roof

Creekside

**❹ Halfway Roof - V3**
Stand start on a sandy jug and follow the seam out the roof. A lower start is possible and as of press time is still a project.

**❺ Unnamed - V7**
Start down in the back of the cave on slopers. Climb up towards the lip on bad left hand slopers and bad right hands to a tricky lip encounter.

**❻ Creekside #1 - V0**
Climb up the left hand side of the face.

**❼ Creekside #2 - V0**
Climb up the center of the face over the water.

**❽ Creekside #3 - V0**
Can you guess? Climb up the right side of the face.

203

# LOS ANGELES COUNTY BOULDERING

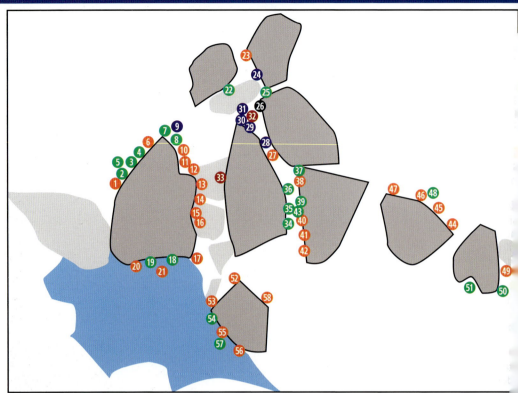

The Main Area is located about 5 minutes downstream of the Halfway area. First boulder you'll come upon is the Zodiac Boulder

❶ **Unnamed - V1**
Climb straight up the right side of the wall.

❷ **Unnamed - V3**
Climb up on decent edges.

❸ **Loaded Bunny - V4** ★
Start sitting on crescent edge. Fire up and right through small edges and crimps to the top.

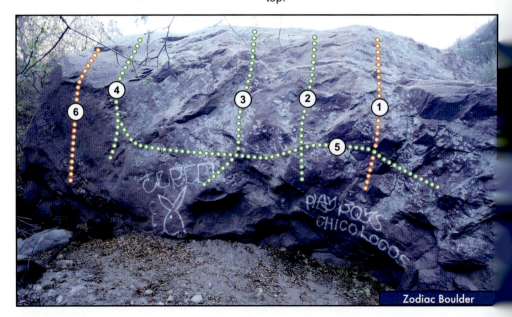

Zodiac Boulder

204

# MAIN AREA - PURPLE STONES

**Beach Face - V3**
t right hand on small cobbles going up
ugh edges and dishes to a rounded top.

**Chico's Locos Traverse - V4**
t at chest height holds to the left of the
nclimb and traverse left to finish up Beach
e.

**Axle Problem - V1** ★
t standing on car axle and go straight up

**Fritz Arete - V6** ★ ★
tart at the blocky arete. Pull up through
gy compression at the bottom and finish
finesse through a lieback sidepull seam to

**Lodestone - V4** ★ ★ ★
w easy moves leads to a committing move
e lodestone. Keep it together and balance
 way to the top along the arete.

**Kung Fu - V7** ★
t with a left hand pocket and a right hand
e. Step up onto the big shelf and huck a
e dyno to the lodestone before continuing
e top.

Zodiac Boulder

Zodiac Boulder

205

# LOS ANGELES COUNTY BOULDERING

Zodiac Boulder

### 🟢 The Motherlode - V3
A variation to Muscle Beach which avoids the large jug hods. Start low on the bulge and climb up via small crimps and a sidepull before joining muscled beach at the big crimp.

### 🟢 Muscle Beach - V1 ★ ★ ★
A rite of passage for the area. Stand start on a little boulder and gain the jug midway up the face to start. Grab a good left hand incut, smear a high right foot and commit. The hardest part is deciding to go for it. Can also be started from low and right from the ground.

### 🟢 Nude Beach - V2
From the hollow flake climb up direct or finish out left.

### 🟠 Downclimb - VB
One of a couple ways off the boulder. A fun climb in it's own right.

### 🟠 Unnamed - V0
Climb up the slab.

### 🟠 The Striated Pebble - V0 ★ ★
Start standing on ramp and go up through small edges through reachy moves to top.

### 🟠 Sandy Beach - V0 ★ ★
Start standing on ramp and climb up through big edges to top.

### 🟠 Pebble Arete - V0 ★ ★
Climb the right side of the arete to the top.

### 🟢 Pebble Direct - V3 ★ ★ ★
Traverse out over the water and then climb upwards via some small quartz crimps and slippery cobble pinches. Don't fall in the water. Arete is off if you want full style points.

### 🟢 Zodiac Direct - V3
Traverse out over the water same as for Pebble Direct but climb up and through the cream colored patch in the dihedral.

### 🟢 Hallucinogenic - V1
Traverse out over the water and go up through purple blobs.

### 🟢 Water Traverse - V1
Traverse from left to right over the water. Can also be done right to left.

### 🟢 V10 Traverse - V3 ★
Start at the far left of the boulder and traverse the length of the boulder to the apex along the lip through slopers and cobbles.

### 🟢 Hawaiian Face - V1 ★
Starts to the Left of Little Hercules. After a tricky mantle to start quest up the tall slab to a couple of exciting moves to the top.

# MAIN AREA - PURPLE STONES

Zodiac Boulder

V10 Traverse

Pungi Sticks

# LOS ANGELES COUNTY BOULDERING

**24 Little Hercules - V7 ★ ★**
Sit start on edges. Hard pulls through crimps/edges lead to an exciting finish as per Pungi Sticks.

**25 Pungi Sticks - V3 ★ ★**
Start standing on boulder with right hand on good incut jug. Pull up to the right facing ledge before liebacking the arete to top. Probably a lot scarier back when the landing was full of bamboo shoots ready to spear you, but the top out still gets your heart pumping. Can also be started from the bottom of the right arete at a grade harder.

**26 Project**
From the blocky feature, traverse up and right along the lip.

**27 Broken Flake - V2 ★**
Climb up the hollow flake to a sloping mantle at the big ledge.

**28 Sandlot - V7**
Sit start and climb straight up through desperate slopers to a good rail.

**29 Purple Squeeze - V7 ★ ★ ★**
Reachy stand start (unless you're an NBA player) on opposing slopers. Squeeze and heel hook your way straight up.

Broken Flake

**30 Purple Prow - V7 ★ ★ ★**
Start sitting on a cobble edge at the base of the arete. Climb up on edges to a block at head height before pressing on up and left through crimps, jugs, and slopers to the top. One of the finest in the Santa Monica Mountains.

Purple Prow

# MAIN AREA - PURPLE STONES

The Naked Edge

The Naked Edge Boulder is home to a more than a half dozen top ropes ranging in difficulty from 5.9 to 5.12+. Most if not all have been soloed or bouldered depending on how you want to classify the ends. These climbs have been excluded from this guide as they are primarily top ropes.

**Purple Prow Direct - V8 ★** ❏
Start same as Purple Prow but head directly up from the mouth/jug midway through the climb.

**Purple Rain - V11 ★** ❏
Start same as Purple Prow, but traverse out to finish the same as Purple Squeeze.

**Ultraviolet - V10 ★** ❏
An improbable start on dime edges leads to a dyno to a rail midway up the climb. Calm your nerves and then make some delicate moves on slopers and pockets to the top. This was put up by Bob Leventhal sans crashpads or rope back in the late 80s and has yet to see a repeat ascent.

**Purple Seedless - V3 ★ ★** ❏
Start standing at blunt arete and climb up left through the dihedral. A low start from under the roof down and left has also been done into this line.

**㉟ Katzy Corner - V4 ★** ❏
Climbs up the shallow corner. Again, a low start from under the roof down and left has also been done into this line.

**㊱ Stepping Stone V2** ❏
Starts just left of the downclimb and climbs up the vertical face.

Purple Seedless

209

Eddie Morillas on Purple Prow  Photo: Joshua Roth

# LOS ANGELES COUNTY BOULDERING

Colorado Boulder

**37 Colorado Arete - V4 ★**
Sit start the arete. Work up the arete, avoiding the adjacent boulder, to the pocket in the face before mantling over.

**38 Pan Am - V2 ★**
Starts standing with left hand undercling seam and a right high pocket. Go straight up.

**39 Corkscrew - V5**
Begin with left hand on pocket and right hand gaston. Grab the russet potato block and try to control the swing.

**40 Key Largo - V1 ★**
Up flakes and pockets to the top.

**41 Large Kilo - V2**
Begin with hands on a sloping horizontal hold. Climb straight up through the shallow corner.

**42 Freebird - V2**
Dyno from big hold to the lip. This route begins on the ground just next to the slab.

**43 Edge Traverse - V3 ★**
Follow the left leaning arete across the formation. Top out at Pan Am.

**44 Unnamed - V1**

**45 Unnamed - V1**
Climb the slab in the center of the face.

**46 Unnamed - V1**
Climb the slab about 4 ft to the left of the arete

**47 Unnamed - V0**
Climb the corner of the slabby face.

**48 Unnamed Traverse - V3**
Traverse right to left along the cobblestone band.

Camp4

# MAIN AREA - PURPLE STONES

Black Knight Satellite

**Take Me to Your Litre - V1**
tart on good edges and climb straight up from e sloping shelf.

**Black Knight Satellite - V4 ★ ★**
arts squeezing a left hand block and a right and edge. A few tricky moves to a hidden ono lead to a exciting move for the top.

**Toxicodendron - V5**
arts sitting on a good left gaston and a right dercling. Climb the dihedral via the arete d crimps. A fall from the top will land you ack dab in the middle of a giant poison oak est.

Toxicodendron

# LOS ANGELES COUNTY BOULDERING

**52 Middle Face - VB ★**
A chose your own adventure climb up the middle of the triangular face.

**53 Purple Pyramid - VB ★ ★ ★**
Climb the right side of the face using the arete, cobbles, and pockets on this easy classic. This climb has been done no hands as well. The trick to the no hands ascent it getting the courage to make a high step.

**54 Pebble Beach - V3 ★**
Climbs a line of cobbles over a shallow pool of water.

**55 Topanga Lieback - V0 ★**
Traverse in over the water from the right side of the wall and then climb straight up to a right facing rail.

**56 Dike Route - V0**
Climb the line of cobbles on the corner.

**57 Traverse - V4**
Traverse the length of the boulder from left to right over the water.

**58 Royal Traverse - V2**
From a crouch start on slopers traverse right through slopers to mantle over at the corner.

Purple Pyramid

Purple Pyramid

# MAIN AREA - PURPLE STONES

Wil Sterner getting started on Asteroid Belt. Photo: Matthew Dooley

# LOS ANGELES COUNTY BOULDERING

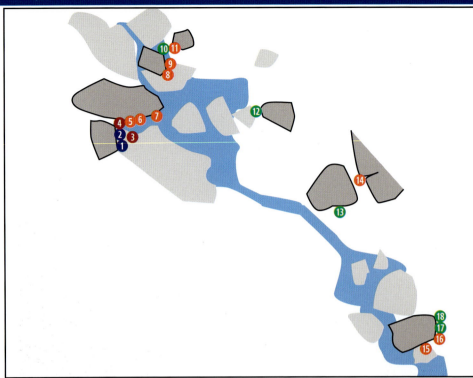

The Whirlpool area can be reached by crossing the stream just south of the Purple Pyramid boulder and then continuing downstream for a couple minutes.

### ❶ Whirlpool Arete - V8 ★ ★
Sit start the arete on a low left edge and an undercling for the right. Climb the arete via pockets, slopers, and hidden holds to the lip before mantling over.

### ❷ Whirlpool Roof - V7 ★ ★
Start on a shallow three finger cobbly pocket and an undercling. Power across to a pocket followed by some tenuous moves to gain the lip.

### ❸ Maelstrom - V9 ★ ★
Start same as Whirlpool Arete and finish on Whirlpool Direct after some tenuous moves to link the two.

### ❹ Hip Replacement - V9 ★ ★
Stand start with a small left sidepull and a right hand sloper. Pull on, go for the lip, and prepare for one hell of a mantle. A lower start seems possible and will significantly up the difficulty. Bring your spotters for this one.

### ❺ Whirlpool Warmup #1 - V0
Start right hand in a jug and go straight up.

### ❻ Whirlpool Warmup #2 - V0
Start right hand in same jug as previous but traverse across the water for ~4 ft before heading straight up.

### ❼ Rinse Cycle - V2 ★ ★
Same start as the warmup #2, but continue to traverse the entire length of the boulder over the water. Don't fall in.

### ❽ Unnamed - V0
Climb up on opposing sidepulls and the arete

### ❾ Unnamed - V0
Climb the right side of the arete up small divo and the arete.

### ❿ Mural - V3 ★ ★
Starts on an undercling pocket and a sloper. few tenuous moves lead you to great edges t the top. Pinball landing.

### ⓫ Dark Comedy - V2
Stand start with right hand in pocket and left hand on the arete. Bust to the top and mant over.

### ⓬ Dimit's Bulge - V4
Starts on good left hand cobble edge and a bad sloper for the right. Make a big move up right to a ledge before following the prow up.

# WHIRLPOOL - PURPLE STONES

Whirlpool Roof

Rinse Cycle

217

Dimitrius Fritz on Whirlpool Roof. Photo: Matthew Dooley

# LOS ANGELES COUNTY BOULDERING

Mural

Dimit's Bulge

DNS Roof

# WHIRLPOOL - PURPLE STONES

Fetal Alcohol Syndrome

### DNS Roof - V5 ★
arts on an undercling right and a left gaston. imb out the roof and top out the crack.

### Fetal Alcohol Syndrome - V0
st done with a hangover to numb the pain d hide the shame. Climb the dirty offwidth to o out into the trees.

### Poprocks - V2 ★
art on the bulb, mantle it, and go to the . Pretty simple, or is it?

### Pebble Crack - V0 ★
mb the pebble riddled crack.

### Chicken Katzatore - V4 ★ ★
ode to Dave Katz. A difficult first move off a sharp crimp (or a sidepull and pocket) gs to you pockets which continue to the

### Asteroid Belt - V5 ★ ★ ★
rt left hand crimp and right hand in a two er undercling pocket. Big moves between de variety of holds with glass feet gets you sloping topout. Finish straight up.

Asteroid Belt

# LOS ANGELES COUNTY BOULDERING

Psychic Over the Phone

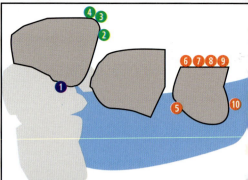

The Banny Boulders can be found a few minutes downstream from the Chicken Katzatore area. Easiest way is to walk along the edge of the east side of the stream until you have to do a little traverse or water crossing. The boulders are just past this.

### ① Psychic Over the Phone - V6 ★ ★
Start matched in the seam. Left hand to a crimp, right to a sloper/pinch and up.

### ② The Grovel - V4
Sit start (really more of a laydown) at the arete and make your way up and over to a blank mantle.

Escape Plan

# BANNY SECTOR - PURPLE STONES

**❸ The Escape Plan - V5 ★**  ❏
Squat start at a low edge for the left hand and a cobble for the right. Slap up multiple times with the left before mantling over.

**❹ The Time Tunnel - V3**  ❏
Stand start on water polished edges. Move up to the lip and beyond.

**❺ Banny's Water Problem - V0 ★**  ❏
Lean over the water to gain the start and then traverse out and over the water before heading upwards.

**❻ Banny Face #1 - V0**  ❏
Climb the right side of the face into the notch.

**❼ Banny Face #2 - V0 ★**  ❏
Climb the middle of the of the face finishing just left of the notch.

**❽ Banny Face #3 - V0**  ❏

**❾ Banny Face #4 - V0**  ❏

**❿ Banny's Bath - V1**  ❏
Traverse out over the water and up.

Water Problem

Banny Face

223

# LOS ANGELES COUNTY BOULDERING

The Guerrilla Field is located further downstream tucked away in a little alcove on the east side of the stream. These boulders are pretty hidden so you'll have to look hard for them. Best way to find them is to walk the stream and keep looking to the left for a spot where the brush opens up a bit in the distance.

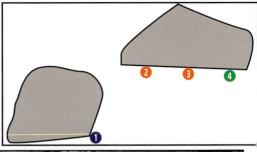

Guerrilla Growth

### ❶ Guerrilla Growth - V6 ★★
Start sitting at a sloper. Keep your balance to gain an anti-cobble in the face before a big move to a pinch at the lip. Follow the arete to the top.

### ❷ The Forbidden Crop - V1
Start sitting at a hole. Move up and left to finish up the dihedral slab.

### ❸ Full Harvest - V1 ★
Climb up through holes and blocks to hidden crimps post the lip for the mantle.

### ❹ Harvest Moon - V3 ★
Sit start on opposing sidepulls/holes. Climb up on sidepulls and anti-pebbles to a deadpoint at the lip. At the lip you can exit left or right at about the same grade.

There are boulders further downstream as well, but those are not detailed in this guide mainly due to their dispersed nature and wandering approaches. While the quality tends to suffer some as a whole and the rocks become smaller and smaller, there are some gems to be found if you're willing to make the extra hike. The Tick (pictured on the next page) is one such gem.

# GUERRILLA FIELD - PURPLE STONES

Full Harvest

Matt Dooley on The Tick. Photo: Paul Dooley

# THE COBBLESTONES

# LOS ANGELES COUNTY BOULDERING

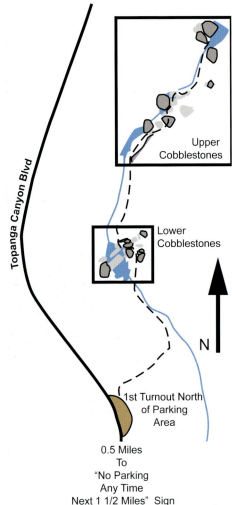

## Overview
The Cobblestones are located in a secluded little canyon right off of Topanga Canyon Blvd about a mile south of the Purple Stones. The boulders are a sandstone conglomerate with cobbles riddled throughout the majority of the climbs. While the holds are not always immediately obvious, the climbing is generally really good once you've figured it out. If no one has been to the area in a while, the path will definitely require some trimming as the grasses around the area grow fast.

## History
The Cobble Boulders are one of the more recent additions to the bouldering in the Santa Monicas, despite them being only about a mile downstream of the Purple Stones. These boulders were initially found and developed by Devlin Gandy in 2009 during a break from the Los Angeles traffic after 45 minutes of bushwacking. The area appeared to have seen some climbing prior to Devlin's discovery, as evidenced by a bolt on top of one of the boulders, but any history of climbing before Devlin's ascents has been lost. Devlin and friends contributed to the majority of the development with Matt Dooley and Garrett Rawlins playing a part in some of the later development.

## Driving
From Pacific Cost Highway, drive north along Topanga Canyon Blvd for a little over 2 miles until you see the "NO PARKING ANY TIME NEXT 1½ MILES" sign. This will be just after the road crosses over the stream. Parking in on the gravel pullout just south of this sign. This parking area can also be reached from the north by taking the Topanga Blvd exit from the 10 and driving south for ~10.5 miles.

## Approach
Once parked, follow Topanga Canyon north staying on the right side of the road for about 0.5 miles until you get to a turnout. This is the first major turnout north of the parking area. At the north end of the turnout there will be a trail leading down to the stream. Once at the water, head upstream until you come across the first boulders.

| VB | V0 | V1 | V2 | V3 | V4 | V5 | V6 | V7 | V8 | V9 | V10 | V11 | V |
|---|---|---|---|---|---|---|---|---|---|---|---|---|---|
| 0 | 6 | 6 | 6 | 5 | 4 | 7 | 3 | 1 | 1 | 0 | 0 | 0 | |

# LOWER AREA - THE COBBLESTONES

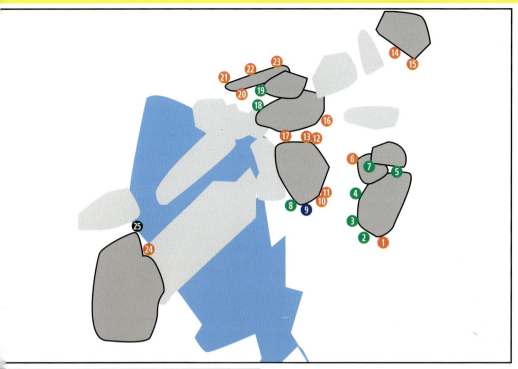

Towers of the Teeth

Vale of Fell Beasts

# LOS ANGELES COUNTY BOULDERING

**1 Towers of The Teeth - V5**
Climbs the tall face.

**2 Vale of the Fell Beasts - V1**
Climbs the series of holes just left of the tree. Be careful as periodically the holes are filled with birds nests.

**3 Morigost - V3**
Starts on an undercling and a pocket. Climbs straight up the face

**4 Spirit Animal - V8 ★ ★ ★**
Starts standing on a right hand 2 finger pocket and a left small pinch. Climbs up through cobbled sidepulls to a difficult finish.

**5 The Constant Gardener - V4**
Climb up the face over the pit.

**6 Lower Bird Law Arete - V2**
Starts low right hand on the arete and a left high on the bulge. An easy move into the big sloper pod leads to a huck to a bad sloper before mantling over.

**7 Upper Bird Law Arete - V1**
Sit start on a black cobble and a flat jug. Climb up the arete before mantling up and over the pit. Can be linked after Lower Bird Law for some multipitch bouldering.

**8 Mirkwood - V5**
From head high pinches, a difficult first move leads to easier climbing to the top.

**9 Gelirwen - V4**
Climbs the center of the tall face from a low start.

**10 Hithlim - V2 ★**
Start standing in vertical pockets on the arete. Balancy moves between sidepulls lead to the top.

**11 Gates of Moria - V5**
Same start as for Hithlim, but climb the face right of the arete.

**12 The Gaffer - V0**
Sit start to the downclimb.

**13 Gollum - V5**
Begins on a left pocket and a sloper at chest height, followed by a long reach out right to a dish and a heel hook to reach up to a positive pocket and the topout. A SDS exists also which starts on a bad undercling pinch.

Spirit Animal

# LOWER AREA - THE COBBLESTONES

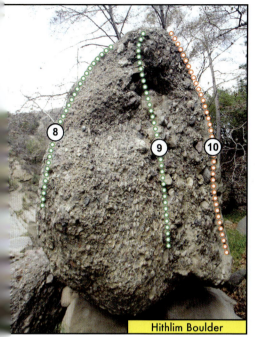

Hithlim Boulder

Hithlim Boulder

Hithlim Boulder

231

*Colin Rosemont on Hithlim. Photo: Joshua Roth*

# LOS ANGELES COUNTY BOULDERING

Sphere of Influence

**⓴ Separation Anxiety - V3** ❑
Starts sitting on cobbles in the middle of the face. A few hard moves gets you to the lip encounter.

**⓯ Sphere of Influence - V5** ★ ❑
Starts left hand on the giant cobble and a right on a wide pinch. Make a couple hard moves to the arete before continuing upwards. Don't cheat by exiting out over the arete.

**⓰ Unnamed - V1** ❑
Climb the arete from a sit.

**⓱ Nananaloch - V2** ❑
Starts standing at edges and climb up the cobble dihedral. Be careful of loose cobbles.

**⓲ Ignoring the Obvious - V7** ★ ★ ❑
Starts low on a shallow three finger pocket and a pinch. Climb up and left via lockoffs between cobbles to a less than ideal top out.

**⓳ Balam - V6** ❑
Starts matched on the lower tier boulder and climbs up through awkward slopers.

**⓴ Project** ❑
Starts off balance between the arete and a poor right hand sloper. Slap your way up the arete without falling into the water.

**㉑ Unnamed - V0** ❑
Climbs the right arete of the tall slab.

Ignoring The Obvious

234

# LOWER AREA - THE COBBLESTONES

Skypager

**Skypager - V0 ★ ★**
Climbs the center of the tall slab.

**Low End Theory - V3 ★**
Start at a low undercling left and a headheight sidepull for the right. Pull up and out the cave then up the face above the corner.

**㉔ The Root Cellar - V1 ★**
Climb the seam to a heads up topout over a horrible landing.

**㉕ Homeless Project**
Climb the dirty face. Maybe with some serious cleaning this would be worthwhile.

Homeless in the Hills

235

# LOS ANGELES COUNTY BOULDERING

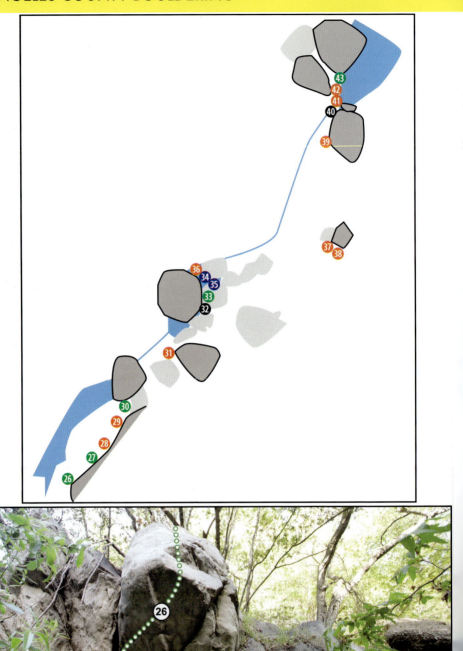

Caveman Squeeze

# UPPER AREA - THE COBBLESTONES

**26 Caveman Squeeze - V3** ❏
Squeeze your way up and over the prow.

**27 Stone Age Struggle - V3** ❏
Climbs up and left from a starting ledge via slopers and slots.

**28 Neanderthal Crack - V1** ❏
Climbs the obvious handcrack.

**29 Neanderthal Safari - V0** ❏
Meander your way up the bedrock from an obvious jug.

**30 John Travolta Memorial Arete - V5** ❏
Starts left hand on the arete and a low right hand. Climbs a few moves up the arete before rocking over onto the face.

**31 Samuel Jackson Memorial Arete - V2** ❏
Climb the arete from a sit start.

Neanderthal Wall

JTMA

237

# LOS ANGELES COUNTY BOULDERING

SJMA

Lizard King

# UPPER AREA - THE COBBLESTONES

Helter Skelter

**Project**
The arete over a bad water landing seems feasible.

**Lizard King - V4**
Starts on low incut cobbles and climbs up the seam in the center of the face.

**Helter Skelter - V6 ★ ★**
Starts on a head high flat edge. A tenuous start leads to a big huck to a good cobbled hold. Continue out right through the jug to the top.

**Helter Skelter Direct - V6 ★ ★**
Same start as for Helter Skelter except exit left after sticking the big move.

**Blackbird Traverse - V0**
Starts on obvious pockets on the right side of the boulder and traverses under the lip to the finish of Helter Skelter.

**Schism - V2 ★**
Start low on a left hand gaston and a right hand edge. Work your way up along the left arete to the boulder's apex.

Schism

239

# LOS ANGELES COUNTY BOULDERING

EIEIO

Hamburger Decoy

**38 Schism Direct - V2**
Same start as per Schism but head straight up the seam.

**39 EIEIO - V4**
Starts on good pockets under the roof. Climb up good edges/pockets.

**40 Project**
If you can ever get a dry landing, a climb up a series of pockets and underclings seems feasible.

**41 Discus - V1**
Starts sitting at the frisbee shaped hold. Climbs up slopers.

**42 Hamburgler - V0**
Sit stat on a shelf at the base of the prow. Climb up via compression.

**43 Hamburger Decoy - V5 ★**
Starts right hand on a good edge and the left on a undercling. A few moves through bad pinches leads to an insecure topout up the prow.

# UPPER AREA - THE COBBLESTONES

# LOS ANGELES COUNTY BOULDERING

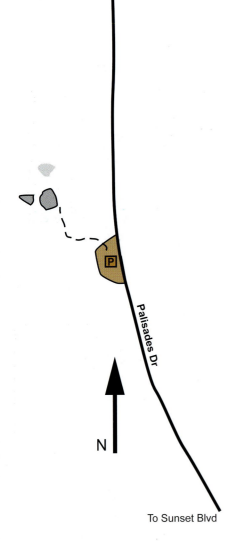

### Overview
Tick Rock is mainly a sport climbing area located in the middle of the Pacific Palisades community, which just so happens to have a couple of boulders scattered around the base of the taller walls. The bould are high quality sandstone and host many variations The rock hosts some of the best quality sandstone i the region.

### History
Limited knowledge of the bouldering development is available for Tick Rock as these boulders were likely an afterthought to those developing the sport climbi here. That being said, it's safe to say Jeff Constine and Abe Etts developed much of the bouldering fou here with Constine doing a lot of excavating in the cave to lengthen the problems found within.

### Driving
From Pacific Coast highway, turn onto Sunset Blvd and head away from the beach (the only way you ca go anyways). Drive along Sunset for 0.8 miles and then take a left onto Palisades Dr. If approaching fr the 405, exit Sunset Blvd and drive 8.2 miles west a then take a right onto Palisades Dr. Once on Palisa Dr, Tick Rock will be on the left after driving north fo 1.4 miles. You will need to drive past the area and take the first u-turn to be completely legal before pa ing along the road at an unevenly paved turnout und a row of tall pine trees. A poorly maintained trail lea up the hill to the boulders.

### Approach
The Tick Rock boulders are located about 100 feet from the road up the steep dirt trail from the parking area. Approach time is less than a minute unless you're crawling uphill.

| VB | V0 | V1 | V2 | V3 | V4 | V5 | V6 | V7 | V8 | V9 | V10 | V11 | V |
|---|---|---|---|---|---|---|---|---|---|---|---|---|---|
| 0 | 5 | 3 | 2 | 2 | 1 | 0 | 0 | 0 | 0 | 0 | 0 | 0 | |

# TICK ROCK

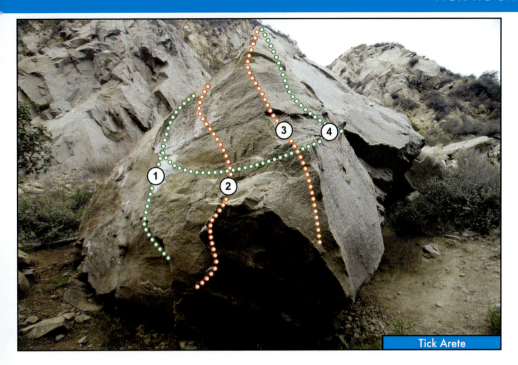

Tick Arete

**Unnamed - V4**
tart on good holds following a left facing corner / roof, climb up the face above.

**Center Face - V1**
egin on the central rib / arete and go up and ght to the top.

**Tick Arete - V2 ★**
imb the obvious arete, the steep start has or footholds but leads to a fun topout.

**Tick Rock Traverse - V3 ★**
averse the boulder in either direction on ality rock.

**Unnamed - V0 ★**
gin at the large holds on the blunt corner ere the boulder turns into the cave. Turn the onto the slab above and top out.

**Unnamed - V0**
gin at the large holds on the blunt corner ere the boulder turns into the cave. Climb and right on big sloping features.

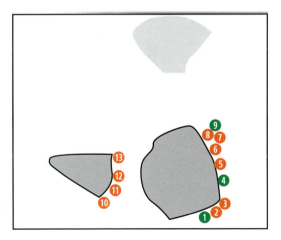

245

# LOS ANGELES COUNTY BOULDERING

Brett Morham on an Unnamed line. Photo: Matthew Dooley

# TICK ROCK

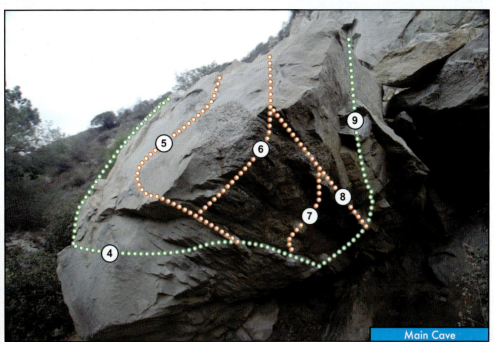

Main Cave

**Unnamed - V1**
tarts low, just left of the deepest part of the
ave. Climb into the diagonal flakes and back
ft to top out.

**Unnamed - V2**
imbs out the cave from the deepest right part
 the cave.  Work up and left on a diagonal
am to great jugs over the lip.

**Unnamed - V3 ★**
imbs out the cave directly up using big slop-
s and rails.

**Thin Seam - V1**
llows the thin crack / seam up the face, the
ete to the right is off.

**Arete - V0**
mbs the arete on the left side.

**Warm Up Crack - V0**
mbs the obvious thin corner and crack.  Su-
r fun and classic!

**Slabby Face - V0**
mbs the slabby face and arete to the right of
 crack.

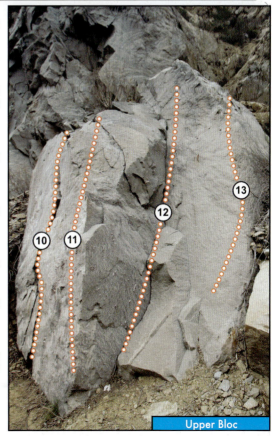

Upper Bloc

# HORSE FLATS

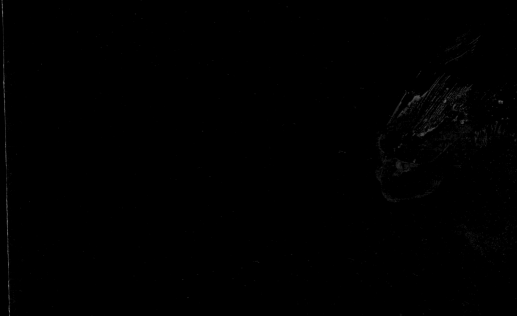

# LOS ANGELES COUNTY BOULDERING

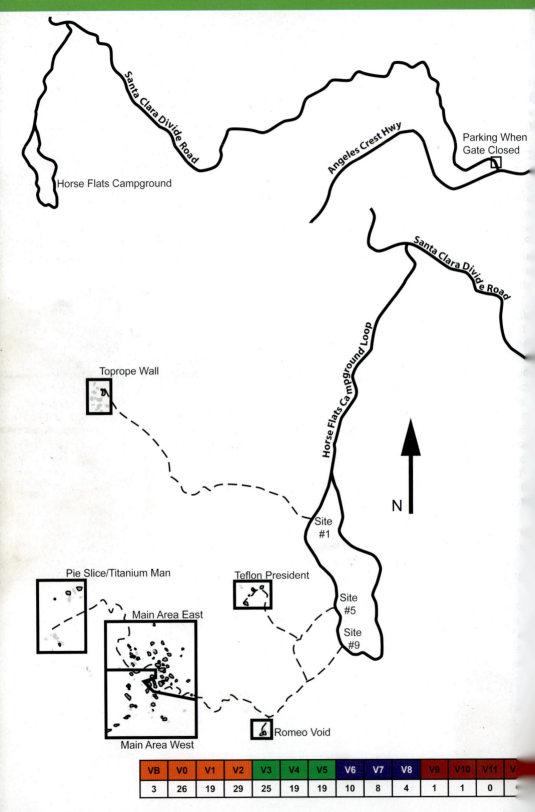

# HORSE FLATS

## Overview

Horse Flats is a region of the San Gabriel Mountains in the Angeles National Forest north of Los Angeles. Horse Flats got its name in the 19th century when Tiburcio Vasquez (of Vasquez Rocks fame in Acton) a known horse thief and bandido used the Horse Flats area as a hide out. Pillaging local towns and ranches during the early 1870s, Tiburcio Vasquez and his gang hid out in the Chilao region. The stolen horses were pastured in the secluded grassland we now call Horse Flats. Vasquez, last of a generation of bandits to operate out of the Southern California backcountry, was captured in 1874 and hanged in 1875. The area is known for its granite bouldering in a semi alpine style area. It is typically open April 1 - November 15 (check with the ranger station to be sure) and is high in the mountains off Angeles Crest Highway at an elevation of 5,700'. The campground is used by both equestrian and non-equestrian campers and is a large loop amongst the sagebrush, Ponderosa pine, and Manzanita consisting of 25 sites. Although there are no grills, each campsite has a fire ring. The fee is currently $12 dollars a day. The high altitude, cool air and solitude lends an aesthetic to the climbing and camping, which is excellent in general. Be aware that the trail is also used by mountain bikers who may be bombing down the trail during your visit

## History

The initial development at Horse Flats was by Keith Lehman and friends in the early 1970's. They mostly did roped climbs but also did some bouldering. In the 1980's Matt Dancy, Mike Ayon and Mike Guardino were the people who brought the area to the attention of the SoCal climbing community. The climbs up at the Toprope area were done by Tony Yaniro and Vaino Kodas but they concentrated on routes, not bouldering. Classics like Yardarm, Bow Spirits, and Teflon President were done in this period. Erik Ericksson lived nearby at the time, and added some stout test pieces as well. A second wave of development by James March and Wills Young in the early 90's added many more problems and saw some truly heinous boulder problems get done. One of the most classic boulder problems in the area was first done by Wills alone on a solo mission when he put up Sword Of Damocles, a beautiful highball arete that takes great skill and a good mind set to do. After the James and Wills surge ended, Horse Flats slowed in development but the adventurous folks will still be able to find new problems. A lot of the climbs here were never named so you'll see a lot of unnamed problems.

## Driving

From the 210 freeway you will take Angeles Crest Highway (2) north for 28.4 miles making a left on to Santa Clara Divide road, which is ~2 miles past the roadside attraction that is Newcomb's Ranch. From here, go another 2.3 miles till you come to the entrance of Horse Flats Campground.

## Approach

There are different approaches depending on which area you end up going to. The Romeo Void, Main, and Pie Slice areas are best approached from the main trail which heads southwest out from site #9-10. Follow this trail uphill anywhere from 10 - 20 minutes uphill to get to the varying areas. The Teflon area is best approached from a trail leading out from Site #5. About a 100 yards down the trail you'll come upon a gully on the right. A quick 5 minute hike up this gully will put you right at the Teflon boulder. The Top Rope Wall has the longest approach and is accessed via a trail leading away from Site 1. After hiking uphill along the trail for ~20 minutes you'll see the big cluster of boulders/walls.

# LOS ANGELES COUNTY BOULDERING

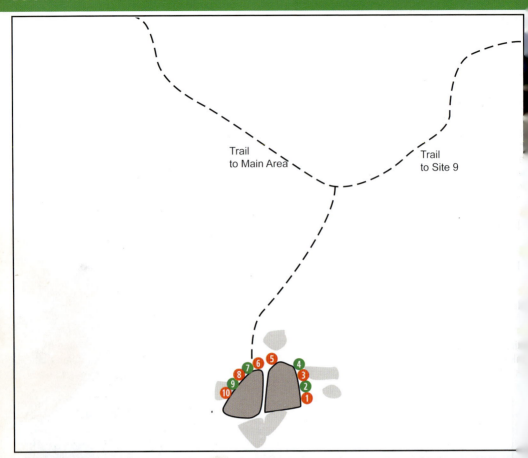

Horse Farts

# ROMEO VOID - HORSE FLATS

The Romeo Void area can be found by taking the main trail which heads downhill from Campsite #9. After about 50 yards you'll cross a small stream before the trail starts it's long climb upwards. After approximately 10 minutes the Romeo Void boulders will be visible off a faint trail leading off to the left. Coming down the trail to the boulders you'll first see the wall which houses Mr. Ed and Ionizer.

**Regular Route - VB**   ❏
Climb the left side of the face.

**Horse Farts - V3**   ❏
Climb the center of the face.

**Credit Card Lover - V1**   ❏
Climb up and along the left facing flake.

**Do Me - V3**   ❏
Climb the face finishing up the right side of the flake.

**❺ Easy Face - VB**   ❏
Climb up the slabby face.

**❻ Talk Dirty To Me - V0**   ❏
Climb the rounded arete.

**❼ Slept Together - V4**   ❏
Start on underclings and climb the face.

**❽ Mr. Ed - VB**   ❏
Climb the very obvious, right leaning crack.

**❾ Ionizer - V3**   ❏
Climb the tall face on thin edges.

**❿ Ed's Route - V1**   ❏
Far right side of the face.

Mr. Ed

# LOS ANGELES COUNTY BOULDERING

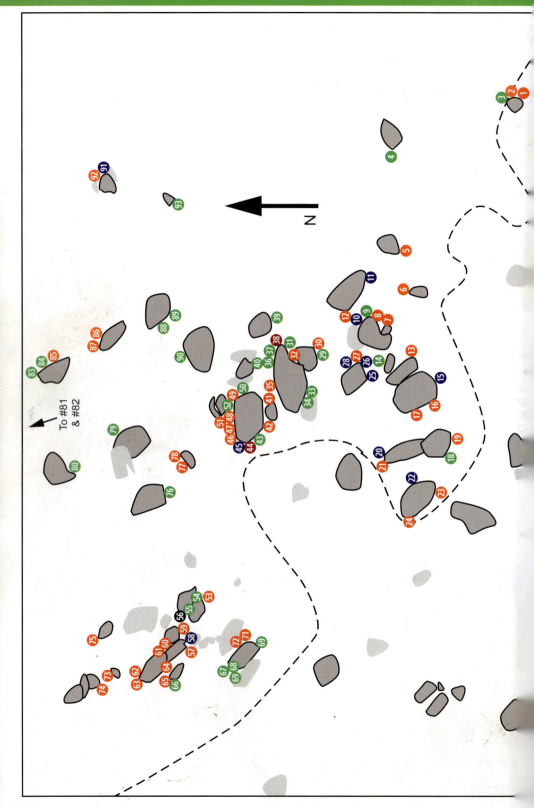

254

# MAIN AREA EAST - HORSE FLATS

Holy Water

Holy Water

The Main Area is reached by following the main trail another 5 - 10 minutes uphill from the Romeo Void Area. You will first come upon the Holy Water boulder right on the trail. Continue along this trail another few minutes up a steep section and you'll see Y Crack on your right once the trail levels back off a little bit. Another 50 yards past Y Crack and you'll be right in the heart of the main area at the classic B1 traverse. The main area is split into two sections: the east and a west section. West section is all to the LEFT of the trail as you hike uphill. East is on the RIGHT.

❶ **And The Son - V2**
Sit start at scoops and climb up the crack.

❷ **In The Name of the Father - V0**
Climb up and right from a dish.

❸ **And The Holy Spirit, Amen - V3**
Sit start on edges. Climb up and right around the corner to a dish.

❹ **Unnamed - V3**
Climb up the rounded arete from a squat start.

Unnamed

# LOS ANGELES COUNTY BOULDERING

Unnamed

Unnamed

Unnamed

# MAIN AREA EAST - HORSE FLATS

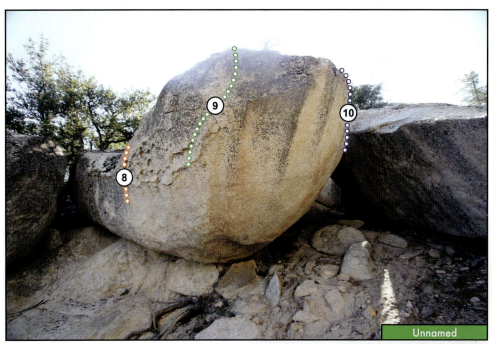

Unnamed

**Unnamed - V1** ★
limb the crack right to topout over the
ulge.  Many variations exist.

**Unnamed - V1**
imb the arete.

**Unnamed - V1**
imb the arete.

**Unnamed - V1**
imb the face on edges.

**Unnamed - V3**
imb the arete from a high start via long
oves.

**Big Man on Campus - V6**
averse through the corridor to top out at the
ulder's apex.

**The Eriksson Problem - V7** ★ ★
mb up the face via sharp crimps and edges.

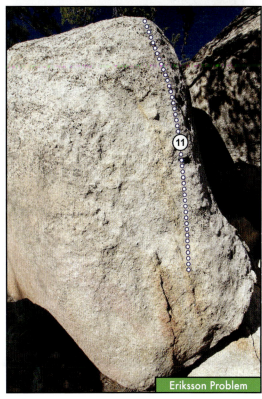

Eriksson Problem

257

# LOS ANGELES COUNTY BOULDERING

Unnamed

Unnamed

# MAIN AREA EAST - HORSE FLATS

Cheek to Cheek

**Unnamed - V2**
Climb the lieback flake starting from underclings.

**Unnamed - V0**
Sang the jug and then climb straight up through the foliage. This climb is located on the boulder just behind Cheek to Cheek in the trees.

**⓮ Cheek to Cheek - V4**
Traverse the lip of the boulder form left to right. Start sitting. End sitting.

**⓯ Arbor Day - V7 ★★★**
Sit start on edges. Climb up and left to a committing topout. Stand start from a jug at chest/head height goes at V5.

Arbor Day

259

# LOS ANGELES COUNTY BOULDERING

Better Bold Than Old

**16 Better Bold Than Old - V0 ★ ★**
Climb straight up via flakes. Tops out left or right over a jumbled landing.

**17 Unnamed - V2**
Jump start from the slab to gain the lip of the boulder before mantling over.

**18 Fish Arete - V3 ★ ★ ★**
Climb the arete to the left of the obvious Y Crack. The climb has sent some would be suitors home with broken bones so be careful.

**19 Y Crack - V1 ★ ★ ★**
Climb the Y shaped crack finishing straight up. Don't cheat out right through the horizontal seam for full points.

**20 Haiku - V7**
Start on underclings and climb up via an horrible right hand pinch.

**21 Unnamed - V1**
Jump to mantle.

Unnamed

# MAIN AREA EAST - HORSE FLATS

Y Crack

Haiku

# LOS ANGELES COUNTY BOULDERING

Belgian Waffle

**㉒ The Belgian Waffle Maker - V6**
Dead hang the lip before mantling up and over. Harder than it looks.

**㉓ Unnamed - V2**
Start high in the middle of the face in a little scoop and climb edges to top.

**㉔ Unnamed - V0**
Climb the obvious flakes. Many variations exist, all of which go at about the same grade.

Swiss Cheese

262

# MAIN AREA EAST - HORSE FLATS

**㉕ With All Due Respect - V6** ★ ❏
Climb the left side of the tall face via a lieback edge and a high middle hold. Tree limbs may make this one a bit interesting.

**㉖ The Sword of Damocles - V8** ★ ★ ★ ❏
Certainly one of the best lines LA County has to offer. Start on crystals in middle of face. Slap out to the arete and then climb up via left hand crimps and right hand arete holds to a harrowing finish. Bring spotters.

**㉗ Unnamed - V0** ❏
Climb the flake from a high start.

**㉘ Red Shouldered Hawk - V8** ❏
Traverse left through slopers before finishing up the lieback flake.

Sword of Damocles

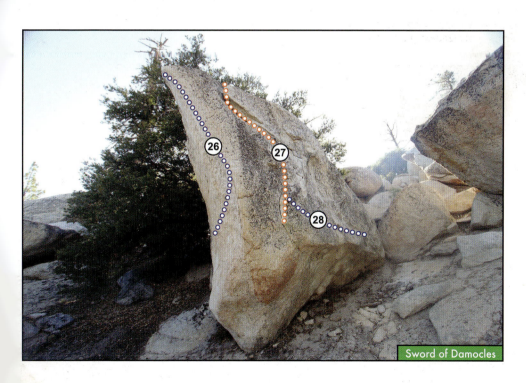

Sword of Damocles

# LOS ANGELES COUNTY BOULDERING

*Lance Carrera setting up for the crux of Sword of Damocles. Photo: Michael Bienek*

# MAIN AREA EAST - HORSE FLATS

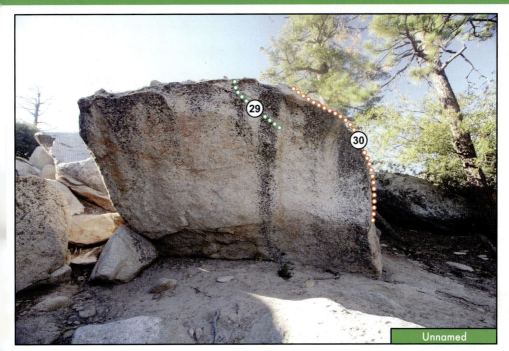

Unnamed

**Unnamed - V3**
From a cheatstone start, climb to top via a right facing edge.

**Unnamed - V1**
Climb the right arete.

**③① Unnamed - V4**
Starting from the bottom corner, traverse up and right before mantling over.

**③② Unnamed - V2**
Climb the short roof starting from flakes from either a right or left start.

Unnamed

265

# LOS ANGELES COUNTY BOULDERING

The Freeway

**㉝ Inner Freeway - V4**
From crimps climb up and left to the lip.

**㉞ Freeway Traverse - V5**
Traverse the lip from right to left.

**㉟ Sloper Problem - V2**
Traverse through slopers.

**㊱ Crooked I - V4**
Start with both hands on decent crimp flake with feet smeared on wall. Climb up and left through edges to a hard finish.

**㊲ The Beer Bet - V5**
Climb up to sloper from a left hand crimp and right hand pinch.

Beer Bet

# MAIN AREA EAST - HORSE FLATS

Blank Generation

**Blank Generation - V10**
sit start matched on a glued on rail. Climb up to a small right hand crimp edge and then make a big throw to a good hold out left before mantling over. It's a glued up mess but still a good problem.

**㊴ The Falcon - V5 ★**
Climb up edges from a sit start at a shelf.

**㊵ Victory Arete - V4**
Climb the right arete via some trickery.

The Falcon

Victory Arete

267

# LOS ANGELES COUNTY BOULDERING

B1 Traverse

**41 Unnamed - V1**
Climb the arete.

**42 Unnamed - V1**
Climb up the slabby face.

**43 B1 Traverse - V5** ★★
Start sitting at the corner and traverse the length of the boulder through a variety of holds before finishing on plates. Stand start at far right goes at V4.

**44 Wills' Dyno - V9**
Start on thin crimps and dyno to the plates out right before continuing to the top.

**45 Sharma Problem - V6** ★
Starting on small knobs climb up and left avoiding large holds out right.

Wills' Dyno

# MAIN AREA EAST - HORSE FLATS

Warmup Face

**Unnamed - V0**
Climb the face on hollow flakes face from a left facing flake.

**Unnamed - V0**
Climb face up edges.

**Unnamed - V2** ★
Climb hollow edges to top.

**49 Unnamed - V2** ★
Climb thin edges up the arete. This one get the blood pumping for sure.

**50 Unnamed - V3**
Starting from obvious edges, dyno to the lip.

Unnamed

*Neal Kaptain on B1 traverse circa 1993. Photo: John Sherman Collection*

# LOS ANGELES COUNTY BOULDERING

Thin Crack

**51 Thin Crack - V1 ★★**
Climb the obvious crack from a sit start. Finish up the crack or bail out right onto the face.

**52 Yen - V5**
Climb the face right of the arete starting off tin holds. Arete is off.

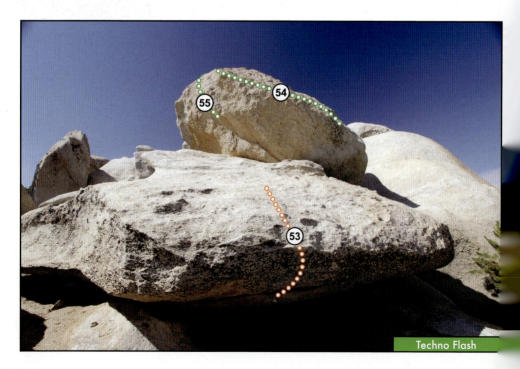

Techno Flash

# MAIN AREA EAST - HORSE FLATS

**㊸ Unnamed - V0**   ❏
Start sitting at a flake/edge. Mantle.

**㊹ Techno Flash - V3**   ❏
Traverse the lip of the boulder from right to left.

**㊺ Your Everyday Junglist - V3**   ❏
Start at high underclings. Make a few harder moves up and left to the lip. Can be done from a sit down and right as well at ~V6.

**㊻ Project?**   ❏
Not sure if this has been done, but a line up the prow seems feasible.

**㊼ Barndoor Arete - V3 ★ ★**   ❏
Climb the arete from a stand start. Exits onto the left face about 3/4 of the way up. Classic.

**㊽ El NinYo! - V6 ★**   ❏
Climb the overhanging arete.

**㊾ Unnamed - V0**   ❏
Sit start at an edge and climb up the corner

Junglist

Barndoor

273

# LOS ANGELES COUNTY BOULDERING

Barndoor Crack

Unnamed

**60 Unnamed - V0**
Climb the crack in the corridor.

**61 Unnamed - V0**
From a sit start at the corner climb out the roof.

**62 Unnamed - V2**
Climb up to slopers.

**63 Wacky Huecos - V2**
From a low right start climb up and left through huecos.

**64 Unnamed - V2**
Climb the tall arete via flakes from a low start.

**65 Krusty The Clown - V2**
Climb up the slabby arete.

**66 Pebble Pinching S.O.B. - V5**
Climb the face using small pebbles.

**67 The Fang - V3 ★**
Start on the giant flake and climb over the bulge via good holds. Pray the fang never breaks off in your lap.

Wacky Huecos

# MAIN AREA EAST - HORSE FLATS

Flake Arete

Krusty

**68 Unnamed - V5** ❏
Start low in back of the cave and climb out to finish up The Fang.

**69 Zach's Roof - V5 ★ ★ ★** ❏
Start the same as above but exit out the right side over a bad landing.

Zach's Roof

# LOS ANGELES COUNTY BOULDERING

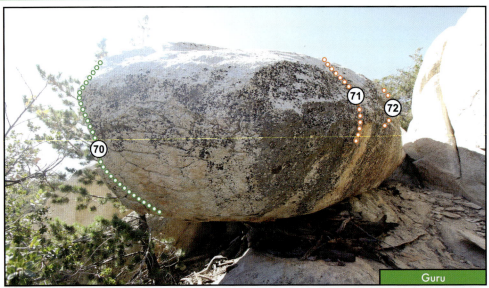

Guru

Coulter Pine Cone

**70 Guru of the Alternative - V4**
Climb the short roof to a mantle.

**71 Unnamed - V2**
Short face problem on the left end of the wall.

**72 Unnamed - V2**
Short face problem in the middle of the face.

**73 Coulter Pine Cone Amnesia - V0**
Climb up and left along the arete.

**74 Unnamed - V2**
Can you say slab dyno? Jump for the xenolit[h] high up on the face opposite of the above pro[b]lem. Someone must have been pretty bored.

**75 Tombstone - V4 ★**
From a low start climb up through right facing small edges. Bring spotters.

**76 The Great Curve - V5 ★**
Climb the curving arete from a standstart. Mantle at the apex.

# MAIN AREA EAST - HORSE FLATS

Tombstone

The Great Curve

# LOS ANGELES COUNTY BOULDERING

**77 Unnamed - V1**
Climb the center of the face via small edges.

**78 Unnamed - V0**
Climb the left arete.

**79 Where Buddhahead's Dare - V4**
A difficult mantle leads to climbing through edges left way off the deck. An ode to Black Mountain's Where Bonehead's Dare.

**80 Springtime - V5 ★ ★**
Mantle into the scoop and then continue upwards. Can also be done as a dyno for the lip after the mantle.

**81 Unnamed - V1**
Climb the arete.

**82 Unnamed - V7**
Climb the face on micro edges. Better bring some serious technique.

# MAIN AREA EAST - HORSE FLATS

Springtime

Unnamed

# LOS ANGELES COUNTY BOULDERING

Bruce Lee

**🥏 Bruce Lee Problem - V5 ★**
Starting in the seam climb up knobs to a sloper before making a dyno to a dish at the lip.

**🥏 Unnamed - V3**
Climb up to and then past the horn starting from the right side of the alcove.

**🥏 Unnamed - V1**
Climb up the seam before trending out and left via huecos to the top.

**🥏 In The Boughs of Hell - V2**
Sit start at the tree and climb up and right.

**🥏 Womb With a View - V2**
Sit start on left facing sloper. Some trickery leads up and right to the finish.

Unnamed

# MAIN AREA EAST - HORSE FLATS

Boughs of Hell

Womb with a View

281

# LOS ANGELES COUNTY BOULDERING

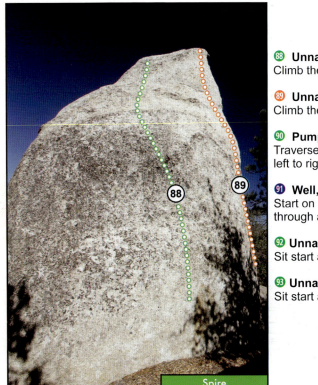

**88 Unnamed - V5**
Climb the thin face.

**89 Unnamed - V2**
Climb the left side of the arete.

**90 Pumpernickel - V5 ★ ★**
Traverse the length of the featured face from left to right.

**91 Well, Do Ya Punk? - V6**
Start on a glued on flake and climb up and left through a small edge. Don't fall.

**92 Unnamed - V1**
Sit start and climb up the face.

**93 Unnamed - V3**
Sit start and climb up the arete.

Spire

Pumpernickel

# MAIN AREA EAST - HORSE FLATS

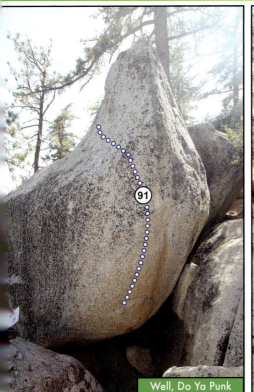
Well, Do Ya Punk

Unnamed

Unnamed

# LOS ANGELES COUNTY BOULDERING

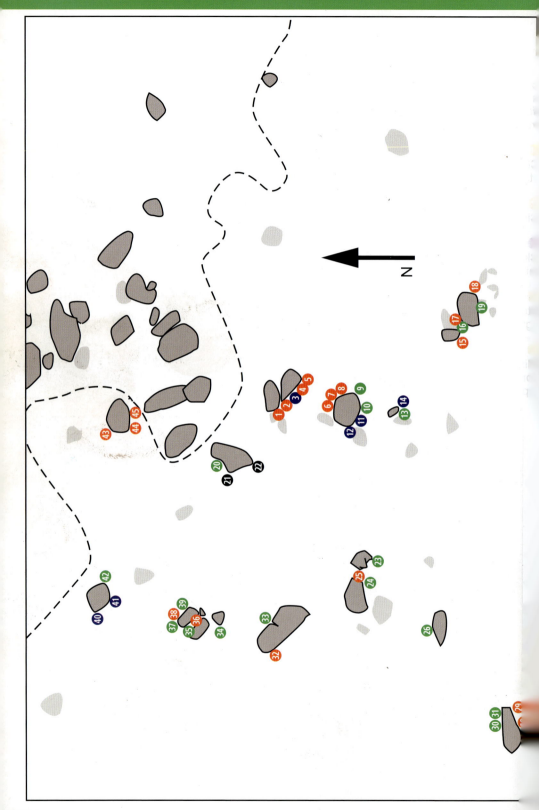

284

# MAIN AREA WEST - HORSE FLATS

Main Area West is located to the left of the trail as you hike uphill. The first boulders mentioned here are located just off the trail downhill from the Y-Crack.

### Unnamed - V0
Climb the face trending up and left from a stand.

### Unnamed - V1
Climb the arete from a stand start.

### Mr. Skin - V7 ★ ★
Climb up and left through a knob. Impossibly thin.

### Unnamed - V2
Step off the adjacent rock and climb up and right along the crack.

### Bow Spirits - V2 ★ ★ ★
Climb the crimpy arete from a stand start. A somewhat awkward start leads to glory jugs at top.

Unnamed

Mr. Skin

# LOS ANGELES COUNTY BOULDERING

Unnamed

Unnamed

# MAIN AREA WEST - HORSE FLATS

Peanut

**Unnamed - V2**  ❏
From right facing sloping edge climb up through slopers.

**Unnamed - V2**  ❏
From a high start climb up and right through ashes.

**Unnamed - V0**  ❏
Traverse left through jugs. Can be done from a sit as well.

**Daddy Longlegs - V4**  ❏
Work your way right using toehooks.

**Unnamed - V4**  ❏
Lieback edges.

**The Peanut - V6 ★**  ❏
Climb straight up from the shelf via big moves on crimps and pinches.

**Nothing but Sunshine - V8 ★ ★**  ❏
From the shelf climb out and left around the edge on edges.

Nothing but Sunshine

287

# LOS ANGELES COUNTY BOULDERING

Unnamed

**⓭ Unnamed - V3**
Climb the arete after starting at the center of the face.

**⓮ Baby Rattlesnake - V6**
Climbs directly up the face on small holds.

**⓯ Unnamed - V0**
Climb the slab opposite of Seams Okay, trending up and left to the apex.

**⓰ Seams Okay - V3**
Climb up to the seam via crimps.

**⓱ The Abyss - V2**
Climb up to good holds after leaning over the chasm to gain the start hold.

**⓲ Unnamed - V0**
Climb the face/arete from a high start.

**⓳ Scrub Jay - V3 ★**
Traverse the lip of the roof from right to left to the midway point before heading up the face.

Unnamed

288

## MAIN AREA WEST - HORSE FLATS

Unnamed

Scrub Jay

# LOS ANGELES COUNTY BOULDERING

Unnamed

**⓴ Unnamed - V4**
Small edges in the center of the face.

**㉑ Project**
From the rail an exit out right looks feasible if it hasn't already been done.

**㉒ Project**
A low start which climbs out the cave looks ripe for the picking.

**㉓ The Dragon Flake - V4 ★ ★ ★**
Go straight up the arete to the flake to a balancy topout. Don't fall! An easier variation which goes at around V1 traverses in from the left via the easy lieback crack/flake.

**㉔ The Satellite Dish - V4**
Mantle into the dish.

**㉕ Unnamed - V0**
From the corner go up and left via the face to finish on the arete.

Unnamed

# MAIN AREA WEST - HORSE FLATS

Dragon Flake

Satellite

# LOS ANGELES COUNTY BOULDERING

Tortoise

*The Tortoise traverse as seen from Dragon Flake*

**㉖ The Tortoise Traverse - V4**
Traverse the length of the rock from left to right ending on top of the tortoise's head.

**㉗ Unnamed - V0**
Easy face climb.

**㉘ Unnamed - V0**
Easy face climb up the center of the boulder.

**㉙ Unnamed - V0**
Climb the arete/face from a stand start.

**㉚ High Chaparral - V5 ★ ★ ★**
Big moves between crimps up the face.

**㉛ Sherman Variation - V7 ★ ★**
Same as High Chaparral but follow the horizontal crack out left before topping out.

# MAIN AREA WEST - HORSE FLATS

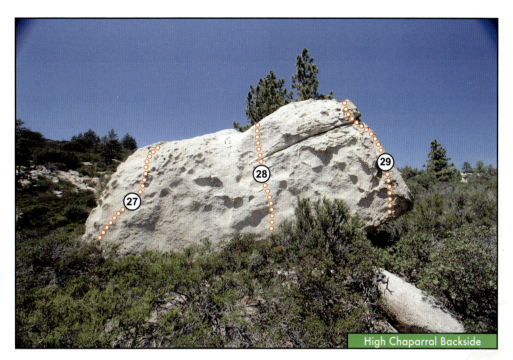

High Chaparral Backside

High Chaparral

# LOS ANGELES COUNTY BOULDERING

Unnamed

Pootchute

150 Lbs

**32 Unnamed - V2**
Climb the crack before exiting onto the face to finish on the apex.

**33 The Pootchute - V3 ★ ★**
Climb the crack.

**34 150 lbs or Under - V4**
From the thin horn climb sloping lieback edges to the top. Pray the horn doesn't pop.

**35 Opposition Movement - V5**
Climb the seam on the right hand side of the corridor.

**36 Unnamed - V1**
Climb the face at the end of the corridor.

**37 The Refrigerator - V3 ★ ★**
Climb the face from a high start (may need a cheater stone). Can also be traversed into from the shelf at the corner at ~V5.

**38 The Defroster - V2 ★**
Climb the large shelves on the corner to a sloping topout.

**39 The Door Magnet - V4 ★**
Dyno through edges.

# MAIN AREA WEST - HORSE FLATS

Opposition

Unnamed

The Refrigerator

# LOS ANGELES COUNTY BOULDERING

Orange Flambe

Christmas Bonus

# MAIN AREA WEST - HORSE FLATS

Unnamed

**Orange Flambe - V8 ★ ★ ★**
From a stand start on a high right hand underling and a left hand edge, climb up and right through the orange face to a spicy topout.

**Christmas Bonus - V6**
Stem your way up the scoop via small edges.

**Unnamed - V5**
Climb the corner.

**43 Unnamed - V0**
Climb the face on good holds.

**44 Unnamed - V0**
Climb the left side of the scoop to jugs.

**45 Unnamed - V1 ★ ★**
A tenuous mantle leads to easier climbing up the face.

Unnamed

297

# LOS ANGELES COUNTY BOULDERING

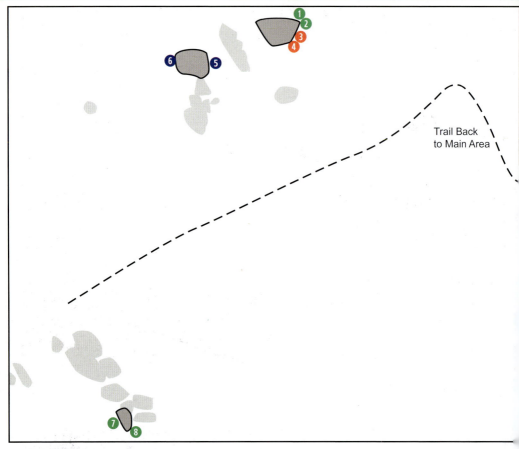

The Pie Slice/Titanium Man areas lie about a 5 minute hike past the main area from the B1 boulder. The Pie Slice boulders lie on the right side of the trail scattered around a tall Pie Slice of a rock which you can see from the trail. Titanium man is just a little further down the trail on the left hand side in another large cluster of boulders.

❶ **Pie Slice Traverse - V5** ★
Sit start on undercling and slot, traverse right out and around corner.

❷ **Gaston Problem - V4**
Sit start on left side of the prow and go left gaston and up.

❸ **Unnamed - V1**
Climb the face a few feet right of the arete.

❹ **Unnamed - V2**
Climb either side of the arete.

❺ **All This Time I Thought I was an Actor - V7**
Start on a glued on flake and climb up and left on small crimps up the face.

❻ **Unnamed - V6**
Climb the overhanging face starting in low pods.

❼ **Titanium Man Traverse - V5** ★ ★
Traverse the boulder from right to left.

❽ **Gutbuster - V5** ★
From a sit climb up to a mantle.

# PIE SLICE/TITANIUM MAN - HORSE FLATS

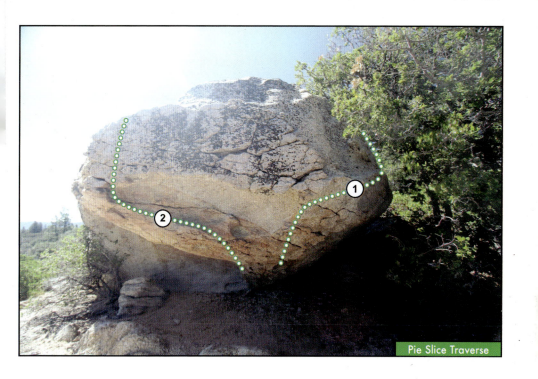

Pie Slice Traverse

Gaston

# LOS ANGELES COUNTY BOULDERING

Actor

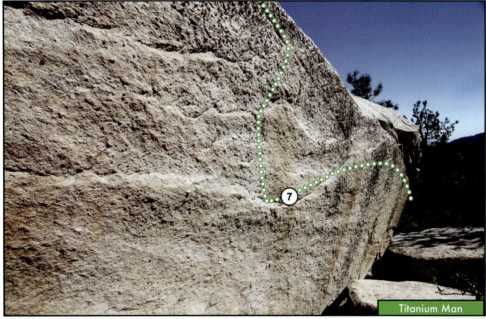
Titanium Man

Gutbuster

# TEFLON PRESIDENT - HORSE FLATS

The Teflon president area is located up a gully to the right of the trail which leads out from Campsite 5. Follow the trail about 100 yards from Campsite 5 and then hike up the gully for a few minutes. If you keep to the gully you'll come up on the backside of the Teflon President boulder.

**1 Unnamed - V0**
Climb the slab in the middle of the face.

**2 Unnamed - V0**
Climb the slab on the right side of the face.

**3 Unnamed - V2**
From a blocky start, turn the corner and go up the face.

**4 Teflon President - V7 ★ ★ ★**
From a stand start, climb up micro edges from the arete to top out at the boulder's apex.

These climbs lie uphill from the Teflon president Arete and are reached via an overgrown trail.

**5 Exterminator - V3 ★**
Climb the thin vertical crack.

**6 Crossfire - V4 ★**
Climb the left side of arete from a high start.

**7 The Gymnasium - V2 ★**
Traverse the boulder from right to left on plates.

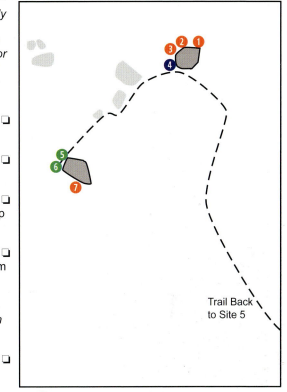

Teflon Slab

301

# LOS ANGELES COUNTY BOULDERING

Teflon President

Exterminator

# TEFLON PRESIDENT - HORSE FLATS

*The Verm grabbing some nonstick surfaces on Teflon President. Photo: John Sherman Collection*

# LOS ANGELES COUNTY BOULDERING

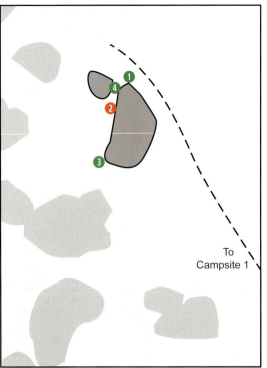

A few of different ways exist to approach the Toprope Area. The easiest is to drive 1/4 mile past the camp ground to Rosenetta Saddle. Hike the trail for about 1/2 mile and make a left when you see the first cluster of boulders. Follow this trail and it will put you at the top of the TR Wall. Walk down and around to the left to get to the base. The second access path is to take a faint climbers trail up across from campsite 1. Follow this trail for about 10-20 minutes and you'll find yourself there amongst giant boulders/walls. The third, and most likely to get yourself lost is to cut directly across the hillside from Pie Slice. A bunch of bushwhacking and faint trails will eventually lead you to the giant cluster of boulders that is the Toprope area. Regardless of which way you take, just keep your eye out for a giant cluster of rock and it's sure to be it.

This area is more known for it's trad climbing and topropes with minimal bouldering at the base. There's some gems out there though if you're willing to put in the work.

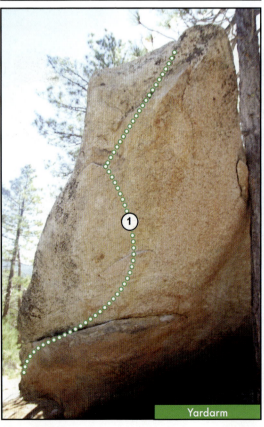

Yardarm

❶ **The Yardarm - V3** ★ ★ ★
From a shelf traverse right and then up the prow to finish on the apex of the boulder an exciting finish.

❷ **The Yardarm Crack - V2** ★ ★
Climb the left leaning crack.

❸ **Unnamed - V3**
Climb the corner from a stand start on a good edge. A lower start from down and right is also possible.

❹ **Unnamed - V3** ★
Climb the tricky slab just behind The Yardarm

# TOPROPE WALL - HORSE FLATS

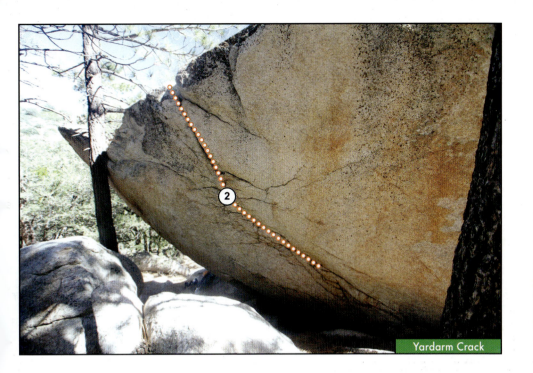
Yardarm Crack

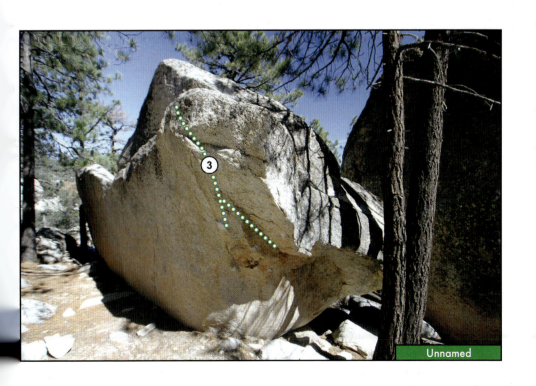
Unnamed

# LOS ANGELES COUNTY BOULDERING

## #

10-40 - V2
150 lbs or Under - V4
5.10 - V1
5.10 Face - V1
5.9 Slab - V1

## A

A-Cups - V6
Abyss, The - V2
Adam's Rib - VB
Addiction - V0 *(D. Fritz)*
Aftershock - V5 *(J. Yablonski)*
AG Pinch, The - V6
Alice in Slanderland - V1
Alien - V5 *(M. Matheson)*
All This Time I Thought was an Actor - V7
Amphitheatre Seam - V3
Amphitheatre Traverse - V2
and the Battle Begun - V2 *(D. Gandy)*
And The Holy Spirit, Amen - V3
And The Son - V2
Anderson Problem - V1 *(P. Anderson)*
Anderson/Johnson Traverse - V7
    *(P. Anderson/J. Johnson)*
Angel Wings - V6
Ankle Grabber, The - V4 *(J. Gutierrez)*
Apes Wall Prow - V2
Apesma Center- V8
Apesma Left - V5
Apesma Rightt – V6
Apparatus - V3 *(B. Leventhal)*
Approach Shoes - V7 *(S. Church)*
Arbor Day - V7
Arete - V0
Arete - V0
Arete - V1
Arete - V2
Arete Me Not - V5
Arete Skeleton - V2
Arock Traverse- V3 *(A. Rock)*
Asteroid Belt - V5
Attack of The Ants - V10 *(K. Shutt)*
Avalon - V8 *(B. Leventhal)*
Axle Problem - V1

## B

B1 Corner - V2
B1 Traverse - V5
Baby Rattlesnake - V6
Bachar Dyno aka Dynamic Duo - V5
Bachar Ladder - V3 *(J. Johnson)*
Bachar Mantle - V5
Backside Warmup - V0
Bad Press - V3
Balam - V6 *(D. Gandy)*
Balancing Act - V3

Banny Face #1 - V0     223
Banny Face #2 - V0     223
Banny Face #3 - V0     223
Banny Face #4 - V0     223
Banny's Bath - V1     223
Banny's Water Problem - V0     223
Barely Legal - V3     85
Barndoor Arete- V3     273
Barndoor Mafia - V2 *(M. Dooley)*     47
Baron Arete - V2 *(C. Baron)*     115
Barracuda - V2     89
Beach Face - V3     205
Beelzebub - V3     104
Beer Bet, The - V5     266
Belgian Waffle Maker, The - V6     262
Beluga Whale - V2     100
Better Bold Than Old - V0     260
Better Than it Looks - V1     109
Big Man on Campus - V6     257
Big Traverse - V1     125
Billy Bob Arete - V2     167
Birdhole, The - V1     163
Birds of Prey - V1 *(B. Morham)*     55
Black Box - V0     69
Black Fly Hell - V8 *(S. Church)*     29
Black Friday- V2     151
Black Knight Satellite - V4 *(M. Dooley)*     213
Black Monday - V2     151
Black Roof - V0     142
Blackbird Traverse - V0 *(J. Roth)*     239
Blank Generation - V10     267
Bleau's Face - V1     126
Blockhead Mantle - V2     85
Blocky - V1     165
Blow - V6 *(L. Carrerra)*     86
Blunt Arete - V1     169
Bob Kamps Face - V0 *(B. Kamps)*     135
Bob Kamps Mantle - V3 *(B. Kamps)*     145
Bold During - V1     154
Bootflake - V3     135
Bootflake Direct - V4     135
Borealis - V0     154
Boulder 1 Traverse - V4     136
Bouldering for Dollars - V3 *(D. Katz)*     91
Bow Spirits - V2     28
Bowling Ball Problem, The - V0 *(B. Leventhal)*     19
Brett's Arete - V0 *(B. Morham)*     49
Broken Flake - V2     20
Bruce Lee Problem - V5     28
Buck and Aron's Dirt Track - V6
    *(B. Branson/A. Couzens)*     10
Buckets to Bag Dad - V3     17
Bulge, The - V0     14
Bull Market - V3     15
Bulletproof Wallets - V3 *(M. Dooley)*     49
Bush Doctor - V3     17

## C

Captain Hook - V9 *(D. Gandy)*     94
Captain's Corner - V0     41

# INDEX - BY NAME

| | | |
|---|---|---|
| Carousel Edge - V1 | 175 | Dangermouth - V1 (M. Dooley) | 52 |
| Carousel Face - V4 | 175 | Dark Comedy - V2 | 216 |
| Carousel Traverse - V5 | 175 | Darkside of the Moon- V5 | 155 |
| Casual Route – VB | 126 | Deadfinger - V9 | 74 |
| Cave Arete - V3 (J. Johnson) | 65 | Defroster, The - V2 | 294 |
| Cave Direct - V6 (J. Johnson) | 65 | Descent Route - VB | 126 |
| Cave Traverse - V10 (J. Johnson) | 65 | Descent Route - VB | 136 |
| Caveman Squeeze - V3 (D. Gandy) | 237 | Desperado - V6 (S. Eaton) | 92 |
| Celluloid Hero - V2 (B. Leventhal) | 77 | Diablo Overhang - V4 | 104 |
| Center Face - V1 | 245 | Digging For Worms - V1 (D. Gandy) | 31 |
| Center Route - V0 | 175 | Dihedral Left - V2 | 137 |
| Centerpiece, The - V5 (D. Fritz) | 199 | Dihedral Right - V3 | 137 |
| Cheek to Cheek - V4 | 259 | Dike Route - V0 | 214 |
| Chicken Katzatore - V4 (M. Lechlinski) | 221 | Dimit's Bulge - V4 (D. Fritz) | 216 |
| Chico's Locos Traverse - V4 | 205 | Discarded Regard - V5 (S. Eaton) | 110 |
| Chimney - VB | 157 | Discus - V1 (M. Dooley) | 240 |
| Chossy Roof - V2 | 126 | DNS Roof - V5 (D. Fritz) | 221 |
| Chouinard's Hole - V2 | 171 | Do Me - V3 | 253 |
| Chouinards Friction Problem - VB (Y. Chouinard) | 155 | Don't Move the Tree - V2 | 117 |
| Christmas Bonus - V6 | 297 | Don't Touch the Banana - V6 | 191 |
| Cleared for Takeoff - V6 (J. Yablonski) | 176 | Door Magnet, The - V4 | 294 |
| Cleft Arete - V1 (S. Church) | 91 | Double Dyno - V5 | 135 |
| Cobble in a Dish - V2 | 86 | Down in the Hood - V1 | 167 |
| Cold Sushi - V10 (D. Vakili) | 181 | Downclimb - VB | 206 |
| Colorado Arete - V4 | 212 | Downclimb – VB | 144 |
| Constant Gardener, The - V4 (L. Carrera) | 230 | Dragon Flake, The - V4 | 290 |
| Corkscrew – V5 | 212 | Druglord - V3 (D. Katz) | 86 |
| Corner Pocket - V0 | 200 | DWP - V2 (D. Katz) | 96 |
| Corner the Market - V3 | 151 | | |
| Corner, The - V2 | 144 | **E** | |
| Cougar Snacks - V2 | 120 | | |
| Coulter Pine Cone Amnesia - V0 | 276 | Ear, The - V4 | 148 |
| Crack Direct - V3 | 149 | Earlobe, The - V5 (D. Fritz) | 115 |
| Crack Hand Traverse - V1 | 183 | Earthquake Face - V3 | 166 |
| Crack, The - V2 | 163 | Earthworm Jim - V3 (D. Gandy) | 29 |
| Crack, The - V3 | 149 | East Canyon Traverse - V3 | 169 |
| Cracksma - V6 | 133 | Easy 1 - VB | 118 |
| Crank Roof - V1 | 74 | Easy 2 - VB | 118 |
| Crank Session or Swim Lesson - V2 (B. Leventhal) | 133 | Easy 3 - VB | 118 |
| Crank Yanker - V9 (D. Vakili) | 133 | Easy Face - VB | 142 |
| Cranking Queenie | 89 | Easy Face - VB | 164 |
| Crawdaddy - V4 (D. Katz) | 91 | Easy Face - VB | 253 |
| Crawfish and Chips - V3 | 31 | Easy Money - VB | 151 |
| Crawl Space - V4 (A. Marcuson) | 253 | Eat Out More Often - V5 | 158 |
| Credit Card Lover - V1 | 203 | Ed's Direct - V10 | 149 |
| Creekside #1 - V0 | 203 | Ed's Route - V1 | 253 |
| Creekside #2 - V0 | 203 | Ed's Traverse - V10 | 149 |
| Creekside #3 - V0 | 164 | Edge Traverse - V3 | 212 |
| Critter Crack - V0 | 94 | EIEIO - V4 (M. Dooley) | 240 |
| Crocodile Rock - V6 (D. Katz) | 266 | Eightball - V3 (M. Guardino) | 166 |
| Crooked I - V4 | 100 | El Diablo - V3 | 104 |
| Cross Step, The - V2 (S. Eaton) | 301 | El NinYo! - V6 | 273 |
| Crossfire - V4 | 52 | ELP - V5 | 148 |
| Crosshairs - V3 (M. Dooley) | 146 | Endo Boy - V3 | 135 |
| Crowd Pleaser - V4 | 193 | Eriksson Problem, The - V7 | 257 |
| Cry Uncle - V6 | | Escape Plan, The - V5 (M. Dooley) | 223 |
| | | Even My Girlfriend Does It - V0 (S. Church) | 115 |
| | | Evenflow - V9 (P. Anderson) | 69 |
| | | Expansion Chamber - V5 | 148 |
| Daddy Longlegs - V4 | 287 | Exterminator - V3 | 301 |
| Daily Circuit - V1 | 172 | | |

307

# LOS ANGELES COUNTY BOULDERING

## F

| | |
|---|---|
| Face - V2 | 152 |
| Face - V2 | 175 |
| Face - V2 | 192 |
| Face #1 - V3 | 111 |
| Face #2 - V1 | 111 |
| Face #3 - V1 | 111 |
| Face #4 - V4 | 111 |
| Face and Crack - V0 | 174 |
| Face Problem - V5 | 185 |
| Falcon, The - V5 | 267 |
| Fang, The - V3 | 274 |
| Fear Factor - V3 | 97 |
| Feel the Rush - V4 *(D. Fritz)* | 115 |
| Fetal Alcohol Syndrome - V0 *(B. Morham)* | 221 |
| Fighting with Alligators - V11 *(Y. Kuperstein)* | 188 |
| Fish Arete - V3 | 260 |
| Flake - VB | 152 |
| Flake to Nowhere - V2 | 164 |
| Flake, The - VB | 144 |
| Flakes - V0 | 190 |
| Flash Me - V3 *(D. Fritz)* | 185 |
| Flyboy - V4 | 103 |
| Flydaddy - V2 *(D. Katz)* | 89 |
| Flying Circus - V4 | 149 |
| Font, The - V6 *(J. Johnson)* | 164 |
| Forbidden Crop, The - V1 *(M. Dooley)* | 224 |
| Fraidy Cat - V2 | 97 |
| Freebird - V2 | 212 |
| Freeway Traverse - V5 | 266 |
| Fritz Arete - V6 *(D. Fritz)* | 205 |
| Fritz Face - V6 *(D. Fritz)* | 165 |
| Frock Problem - V6 *(D. Fritz)* | 92 |
| Full Harvest - V1 *(W. Sterner)* | 224 |
| Full Powder - V6 | 85 |
| Full Throttle - V7 | 85 |

## G

| | |
|---|---|
| Gaffer, The - V0 *(J. Roth)* | 230 |
| Game of Death - V3 *(M. Dooley)* | 55 |
| Garrett's Pit Problem - V2 *(G. Rawlins)* | 200 |
| Gaslight Lantern - V5 *(E. Gia)* | 199 |
| Gaston Problem - V4 | 298 |
| Gastoning - V5 *(P. Anderson)* | 135 |
| Gates of Moria - V5 *(D. Gandy)* | 230 |
| Gato Cosmico - V9 *(F. Langbehn)* | 118 |
| Gelirwen - V4 *(D. Gandy)* | 230 |
| Ghetto Bird - V5 *(S. Josif)* | 141 |
| Giant Step Unfold - V3 *(B. Leventhal)* | 96 |
| Glass Animals - V1 *(M. Dooley)* | 53 |
| Gold Rush - V6 *(N. LeProhon)* | 115 |
| Goldfinger - V6 *(D. Fritz)* | 117 |
| Gollum - V5 *(D. Gandy)* | 230 |
| Gomer Pile - V3 | 141 |
| Great Curve, The - V5 | 276 |
| Grimace - V1 *(B. Morham)* | 55 |
| Grip Grand - V4 *(M. Dooley)* | 54 |
| Grovel, The - V4 *(M. Dooley)* | 222 |

| | |
|---|---|
| Guar Scar - V3 *(M. Guardino)* | 166 |
| Guarglaphone - V6 *(M. Guardino)* | 185 |
| Guerilla Growth - V6 *(M. Dooley)* | 224 |
| Guru of the Alternative - V4 | 276 |
| Gutbuster - V5 | 298 |
| Gutterball - V2 | 67 |
| Gutterball Left Face - V0 | 67 |
| Gutterball Middle Face - V0 | 67 |
| Gymnasium, The - V2 | 301 |

## H

| | |
|---|---|
| Haiku - V7 | 260 |
| Half Gram - V3 | 171 |
| Halfway Roof - V3 *(M. Dooley)* | 203 |
| Hallucinogenic - V1 | 206 |
| Hamburger Decoy - V5 *(E. Gia)* | 240 |
| Hamburgler - V0 *(M. Dooley)* | 240 |
| Han Shan Arete - V4 | 63 |
| Hand Crack - V3 | 179 |
| Harder Than It Looks - V4 | 97 |
| Harmonica Lewinsky - V5 *(M. Dooley)* | 202 |
| Harvest Moon - V3 *(M. Dooley)* | 224 |
| Hawaiian Face - V1 | 206 |
| Hawk, The - V3 | 188 |
| Headwaters Arete - V4 *(D. Fritz)* | 198 |
| Headwaters Ramp - V0 | 198 |
| Headwaters Traverse - V4 *(W. Sterner)* | 198 |
| Hedgeclipper - V2 | 165 |
| Hein Flake - V3 | 185 |
| Helter Skelter - V6 *(D. Gandy)* | 239 |
| Helter Skelter Direct - V6 *(D. Gandy)* | 239 |
| Hieroglyphics - V4 *(S. Church)* | 117 |
| High Chaparral - V5 | 292 |
| Hip Replacement - V9 *(E. Gia)* | 216 |
| Hithlim - V2 *(D. Gandy)* | 230 |
| Hog Tied - V3 | 148 |
| Hollowman - V1 *(M. Dooley)* | 47 |
| Holy Shit - V1 | 172 |
| Hood, The | 167 |
| Hoof and Mouth - V2 | 145 |
| Horse Farts - V3 | 253 |
| Hot Rod - V0 | 85 |
| Hot Tuna - V5 | 181 |
| Huevos - V10 *(F. Langbehn)* | 74 |
| Hungarian Traverse - V4 *(T. Veru)* | 106 |
| Hypodermic - V2 *(S. Church)* | 115 |

## I

| | |
|---|---|
| If You Dare - V7 *(J. Johnson)* | 65 |
| Ignoring the Obvious - V7 *(W. Ureda)* | 23 |
| Illuminati - V1 | 20 |
| In The Boughs of Hell - V2 | 28 |
| In The Name of the Father - V0 | 25 |
| Inbetweener, The - V4 *(L. Carrera)* | 19 |
| Incubus - V4 *(B. Leventhal)* | 16 |
| Inner Freeway - V2 | 26 |
| Inside Out - V4 | 14 |
| Intimidation - V3 | 10 |

# INDEX - BY NAME

| | | | |
|---|---|---|---|
| Ionizer - V3 | 253 | Loaded Bunny - V4 | 204 |
| Island Boulder Traverse - V3 *(D. Katz)* | 106 | Lodestone - V4 *(J. Long)* | 205 |
| Islands in the Stream - V3 *(D. Katz)* | 109 | Lord of the Flies - V3 *(W. Ureda)* | 29 |
| It Only Takes One Finger - V5 *(D. Fritz)* | 118 | Lost In Space - V1 | 86 |
| It's Nyaaat Easy - V5 *(S. Estren)* | 33 | Lost Keys Arete - V1 *(M. Dooley)* | 49 |
| | | Lost Keys of God - V6 *(M. Dooley)* | 49 |
| **J** | | Low and Behold - V8 *(P. Anderson)* | 141 |
| | | Low End Theory - V3 *(G. Rawlins)* | 235 |
| Jake's Face - V1 | 126 | Lower Bird Law Arete - V2 *(M. Dooley)* | 230 |
| Jam Crack - V1 | 193 | Lucky Strike - V2 *(M. Dooley)* | 49 |
| Jam Crack – VB | 133 | Luckyman - V0 *(B. Leventhal)* | 109 |
| Jaws - V1 | 190 | Lunge or Plunge - V4 *(M. Fekkes)* | 77 |
| Jingus - V2 | 171 | Lunker, The - V0 | 69 |
| John Travolta Memorial Arete - V5 *(D. Gandy)* | 237 | Lycra Boy - V2 | 104 |
| Johnson Arete - V4 *(J. Johnson)* | 155 | Lycra Linkup - V8 | 104 |
| Johnson Mantle - V6 *(J. Johnson)* | 185 | Lycra Man - V3 | 104 |
| Johnson Problem - V6 *(J. Johnson)* | 157 | Lycrabolic - V8 *(D. Gandy)* | 104 |
| Juan Carlo Problem - V1 | 143 | Lycraverse - V8 *(D. Gandy)* | 104 |
| Jump Problem - V2 *(B. Leventhal)* | 92 | Lynn Hill Problem - V7 *(L. Hill)* | 158 |
| Jumping for Mantles- V2 | 92 | | |
| Junky - V4 *(D. Fritz)* | 115 | **M** | |
| Junky Roof - V1 | 126 | | |
| | | Madvilliany - V5 *(M. Dooley)* | 53 |
| **K** | | Maelstrom - V9 *(D. Vakili)* | 216 |
| | | Maggie's Face - V1 | 126 |
| Kaptain Traverse - V4 *(N. Kaptain)* | 69 | Maggie's Traverse - V1 | 180 |
| Katzy Corner - V4 | 209 | Malibu Lieback - V1 | 96 |
| Kerwin Problem Left - V3 *(K. Klein)* | 74 | Malibu Roof aka Chubbs - V11 *(I. Green)* | 65 |
| Kerwin Problem Right - V3 *(K. Klein)* | 74 | Man in the Moon - V2 | 86 |
| Key Largo - V1 | 212 | Mantle - V0 | 94 |
| Kingpin - V4 *(D. Katz)* | 86 | Mantle - V0 | 198 |
| Kodas Corner - V3 *(V. Kodas)* | 167 | Mantle - VB | 118 |
| Kodiak Corner - V3 *(M. Oliphant)* | 164 | Mantle Problem - V0 *(M. Dooley)* | 33 |
| Krusty The Clown - V2 | 274 | Mantle Problem - V5 | 175 |
| Kuan Chin Roof - V4 | 63 | Mantlelobotomy - V1 | 164 |
| Kung Fu - V7 *(S. Eaton)* | 205 | Maple Canyon Arete - V3 *(B. Leventhal)* | 199 |
| | | Martian's Landing Crack - V3 *(T. Yaniro)* | 126 |
| **L** | | Master of Reality - V5 | 148 |
| | | Masters Chamber - V5 | 148 |
| Lance's Problem - V5 | 143 | Matt's Face - V2 *(M. Oliphant)* | 169 |
| Landing Not Included - V7 *(D. Fritz)* | 107 | Mazzi Corner - V2 *(M. Fekkes)* | 166 |
| Landing Not Required - V0 | 107 | Meatgrinder Mantle - V0 | 152 |
| Large Kilo - V2 | 212 | Mickey Mouse - V5 | 181 |
| Largonaut - V4 *(J. Long)* | 176 | Microscope - V6 *(B. Leventhal)* | 165 |
| Laundryroom Innuendo - V1 *(B. Morham)* | 49 | Middle Face - VB | 214 |
| Le Coif- V5 | 85 | Midsummer's Daydream - V3 *(S. Church)* | 92 |
| Leah - V8 *(Y. Kuperstein)* | 120 | Mike's Up Problem - V0 *(M. Waugh)* | 142 |
| Leaping Lizard - V4 *(J. Johnson)* | 136 | Miniholland Traverse - V5 | 41 |
| Left Arete - V3 | 190 | Mirkwood - V5 *(M. Dooley)* | 230 |
| Left of Arete - V1 | 115 | Mommy's Boy Center- VB | 190 |
| Left Problem - VB | 168 | Mommy's Boy Left - VB | 190 |
| LeProhon Press - V3 *(N. LeProhon)* | 96 | Mommy's Boy Right - V2 | 190 |
| Life Is Short - V2 *(D. Gandy)* | 31 | Monkey Paw aka Kate Moss - V5 *(M. Dooley)* | 52 |
| Lion's Head #1 - V3 | 151 | Monos - V2 | 103 |
| Lion's Head #2 - V4 | 151 | Morigost - V3 *(D. Gandy)* | 230 |
| Lo Turn, The - V2 | 103 | Mosaic Thump | 158 |
| Little Hercules - V7 *(W. Ureda)* | 208 | Motherlode, The - V3 *(W. Sterner)* | 206 |
| Little House on the Prairie - V4 *(M. Dooley)* | 57 | Mozart's Traverse - VB | 179 |
| Little Traverse - V0 | 125 | Mr. Ed - VB | 253 |
| Lizard King - V4 *(S. Church)* | 239 | Mr. Skin - V7 | 285 |
| | | Mural - V3 *(M. Dooley)* | 216 |

# LOS ANGELES COUNTY BOULDERING

Muscle Beach - V1     206
Mutiny - V3
My Boy Bleau - V2 (D. Fritz)

## N

Naked Man Overboard - V3 (G. Rawlins)
Nananaloch- V2 (M. Roth)
Natural, The - V7 (D. Fritz)
Neal Kaptain's Horror - V8
Neanderthal - V3 (J. Roth/K. Baker)
Neanderthal Crack - V1 (M. Dooley)
Neanderthal Safari - V0 (D. Gandy)
Neckbeard Aficionado - V2 (M. Dooley)
Niagara Arete - V1 (M. Guardino)
Niagara Fist - V2 (M. Guardino)
Night Train - V8 (M. Reardon)
Niles Reardon Traverse - V2
No Honor Amongst Thieves - V9
    (F. Langbehn/D. Gandy)
North Face - V5
North Face - VB
North Face Flake - VB
North Face Pump Rock - V0
Northwest Face - V2
Northwest Face - VB
Nose Arete - VB
Nose Dive - V5
Nothing but Sunshine - V8
Nude Beach - V2
Number Nine - V0
Nylon Boy - V4

## O

Oasis - V3 (D. Katz)
Oasis Arete - V1
Oasis Seam - V1
Ode to the West Wind - V5 (D. Gandy)
Off The Tree - V2 (M. Bailey)
Offwidth - V4
Old Man and the Point - V7 (D. Fritz)
Old Skool Cool - V3
Opposition Movement - V5
Orange Flambe - V8
Over Lord - V4 (B. Leventhal)
Over the Hoof - V3
Ozone Factor- V1

## P

Pablo Escobar - V7 (D. Fritz)
Pai Mei Overhang - V5
Pan Am - V2
Pancake - V4
Paranoia - V5 (M. Dooley)
Peanut, The - V6
Pebble Arete - V0
Pebble Beach - V3 (B. Leventhal)
Pebble Crack - V0

Pebble Direct - V3     206
Pebble Pinching S.O.B. - V5     274
Pie Slice - V1     154
Pie Slice Traverse - V5     298
Pile Driver- V3     141
Pile Lieback - V2     141
Pile Ups Mantle - V2     141
Pile Ups Traverse - V2     141
Pinball - V5 (D. Fritz)     103
Pink Floyd - V4     149
Pipe Dream - V2     86
Pit Arete - V2 (S. Church)     91
Pit Problem - V0 (S. Church)     91
Planet of The Apes Traverse - V5     62
Pliers - V2     145
Plunger - V6 (J. Johnson)     168
Pocket Face - V0     171
Pocket Protector - V1 (B. Morham)     49
Pocket Traverse - V2     192
Pocketed Overhang - V2     86
Point Blank     144
Pootchute, The - V3     294
Poprocks - V2 (M. Bowling)     221
Potato Chip - V7     191
Potholes Face #1 - V0     144
Potholes Face #2 - V0     144
Potholes Traverse - V2     161
Powder Edge - V3 (D. Katz)     85
Power to the People - V2     103
Powerbeast - V3 (B. Leventhal)     77
Procrastinator - V3 (D. Katz)     86
Prow - V2     66
Prow SDS, The - V12 (F. Langbehn)     94
Prow, The - V3     94
Psychic Over the Phone - V6 (A. Rothner)     222
Puggie - V0     166
Pump Arete - V1     135
Pump Rock Traverse - V3     135
Pumpernickel - V5     282
Pungi Sticks - V3     208
Purple Haze Traverse - V4 (L. Carrera)     200
Purple Heart - V6 (M. Reardon)     74
Purple People Eater - V9     202
Purple Prow - V7 (D. Fritz)     208
Purple Prow Direct - V8 (D. Gandy)     209
Purple Pyramid - VB     214
Purple Rain - V11 (D. Gandy)     209
Purple Seedless - V3     209
Purple Squeeze - V7 (D. Gandy)     208

## Q

Quickstep - V2     17

## R

Radulator, The - V3     16
Rafiki's Tomb - V4 (M. Dooley)     54
Railed Out - V4     11
Ramada - V3     14

# INDEX - BY NAME

|  |  |
|---|---|
| Reach #1 - V4 | |
| Reach #2 - V3 | |
| Real Crystal Ball Mantle, The - V6 | |
| Real Yabo Mantle, The - V4 *(J. Yablonski)* | |
| Reardon's Problem - V5 *(M. Reardon)* | |
| Rebel Yell - V2 | |
| Recluse Roof - V4 *(P. Anderson)* | |
| Recycle - V5 | |
| Recycler, The - V4 *(M. Dooley)* | |
| Red Shouldered Hawk - V8 | |
| Red Spot - V2 *(D. Fritz)* | |
| Refrigerator, The - V3 | |
| Reggae Route - V1 | |
| Regular Route - VB | |
| Renaissance Man - V2 | |
| Revolt - V2 | |
| Riceball - V5 | |
| Right Arete - V2 | |
| Right Problem - VB | |
| Rinse Cycle - V2 *(M. Dooley)* | |
| River Arete - V1 *(S. Church)* | |
| Roadkill - V8 *(E. Gia)* | |
| Roadkill Direct - V9 *(E. Gia)* | |
| Roadside Traverse - V3 | |
| Rock Lobster - V2 *(D. Katz)* | |
| Rodeo Style - V2 | |
| Rollercoaster - V2 | |
| Roof Crack - V4 | |
| Root Cellar, The - V1 *(M. Dooley)* | |
| Route Rustlin' - V1 | |
| Router Bit - V5 | |
| Royal Traverse - V2 *(M. Dooley)* | |
| Sacking of Rome, The - V5 | |
| Samsquatch - V7 *(S. Eaton)* | |
| Samuel Jackson Memorial Arete - V2 *(D. Gandy)* | |
| Sandbox Traverse, The - V6 | |
| Sandlot - V7 *(L. Carrera)* | |
| Sandlow Problem - V5 *(A. Sandlow)* | |
| Sandy Beach - V0 | |
| Satellite Dish, The - V4 | |
| Save The Best for Last - V7 *(D. Fritz)* | |
| Say Goodnight - V6 | |
| Scary Face - V4 | |
| Schism - V2 *(G. Rawlins)* | |
| Schism Direct - V2 *(G. Rawlins)* | |
| Scoopless - V3 | |
| Scoops - V0 *(S. Eaton)* | |
| Scorpion - V5 *(M. Oliphant)* | |
| Scrambled Eggs Traverse - V3 | |
| Scrub Jay - V3 | |
| Sculpture's Eliminate - V5 | |
| Sculpture's Traverse - V3 | |
| Seam - V2 | |
| Seam Stealer - V6 | |
| Seam, The - V4 *(B. Leventhal)* | |
| Seamless - V4 *(S. Eaton)* | |
| Seams Okay - V3 | |
| Semi-Rad - V0 *(M. Dooley)* | |
| Separation Anxiety - V3 *(G. Rawlins)* | 234 |
| Sharkfin - V0 | 106 |
| Sharma Problem - V6 | 268 |
| Sherman Variation - V7 | 292 |
| Shit Crystal - V1 | 103 |
| Short Story - V0 | 135 |
| Shorty Shea - V0 | 163 |
| Shot's Fired - V6 *(S. Church)* | 117 |
| Sierra Face - VB | 143 |
| Sierra Traverse - V5 | 143 |
| Silent Running - VB | 144 |
| Skidmarks - V3 *(S. Church)* | 118 |
| Skypager - V0 *(M. Dooley)* | 235 |
| Slab - V1 | 100 |
| Slabby Face - V0 | 247 |
| Slanderland - V4 | 172 |
| Slant Flake - V1 | 137 |
| Slant Rock Face Center - VB | 137 |
| Slant Rock Face Left - VB | 137 |
| Slant Rock Face Right - VB | 137 |
| Slap - V1 | 155 |
| Slap Happy Left - V2 | 104 |
| Slap Happy Right - V2 | 105 |
| Slapshot - V3 | 105 |
| Sleazy Tabloid - V0 | 172 |
| Sledgehammer - V4 | 141 |
| Slept Together - V4 | 253 |
| Slide, The - V1 | 94 |
| Slime - V3 | 145 |
| Slop Arete - V2 *(M. Dooley)* | 47 |
| Sloper Problem - V2 | 266 |
| Small Fry - V2 | 103 |
| Small with Big Consequences - V2 *(D. Fritz)* | 97 |
| Snot Here aka Powerglide - V6 | 158 |
| Soapstone Traverse - V5 *(S. Church)* | 199 |
| Sole Food - V0 | 85 |
| Sole Power - VB | 85 |
| Sole Sister - VB | 85 |
| South America Face - VB | 66 |
| South Face Overhang | 171 |
| Southeast Arete - VB | 145 |
| Southeast Corner - V2 | 136 |
| Southwest Corner - V0 | 175 |
| Southwest Corner - V1 | 171 |
| Spencer's Prow - V2 *(S. Church)* | 103 |
| Spencer's Roof - V4 *(S. Church)* | 200 |
| Spencer's Tree Problem - V3 *(S. Church)* | 96 |
| Sphere of Influence - V5 *(M. Dooley)* | 234 |
| Spiral Direct - V3 | 154 |
| Spiral Direct II - VB | 154 |
| Spiral Traverse - V3 | 154 |
| Spirit Animal - V8 *(M. Dooley)* | 230 |
| Split Crack - V0 | 171 |
| Split Decision - V3 *(B. Leventhal)* | 157 |
| Splitter Choss - V0 *(B. Morham)* | 57 |
| Spongebob - V7 *(M. Reardon)* | 73 |
| Springtime - V5 | 278 |
| Squirrel Head Roof - V5 *(D. Fritz)* | 115 |
| Squirrel Head Traverse - V3 | 117 |
| Standard Route - V2 | 158 |
| Static Lizard - V4 | 136 |

311

# LOS ANGELES COUNTY BOULDERING

| | |
|---|---|
| Stepping Stone - V2 | |
| Sticky Fingers - V2 | |
| Stone Age Struggle - V3 *(D. Gandy)* | |
| Street Legal - V1 | |
| Street Legal - V2 | |
| Striated Pebble, The - V0 | |
| Stuffed LeProhon - V3 *(N. LeProhon)* | |
| Sudden Impact - V6 | |
| Sugar Daddy - V0 | |
| Sugar Pops - V3 | |
| Super Natural - V5 *(J. Johnson)* | |
| Swig's Alcove - V3 *(M. Dooley)* | |
| Swim Wear - V2 *(M. Lechlinski)* | |
| Sword of Damocles, The - V8 *(W. Young)* | |

## T

| | |
|---|---|
| T2 - V5 | |
| Take Me to Your Litre - V1 *(B. Morham)* | 86 |
| Talibanny - V1 | 213 |
| Talk Dirty To Me - V0 | 200 |
| Techno Flash - V3 | 253 |
| Teflon - V4 | 273 |
| Teflon President - V7 | 106 |
| Temporal Relativity - V6 *(D. Gandy)* | 301 |
| Tension - V3 | 29 |
| Terminator - V7 *(D. Katz)* | 103 |
| Test Tube - VB | 86 |
| Tête-à-Tête - V5 *(D. Gandy)* | 97 |
| Texas Flake - V0 | 109 |
| Texas Flake Arete - V1 | 181 |
| Thaw Dyno - V4 *(K. Thaw)* | 181 |
| There's Something in the Bushes - V5 *(S. Church)* | 142 |
| Thimble of The Santa Monicas, The - V5 *(D. Fritz)* | 120 |
| Thin Crack - V1 | 198 |
| Thin Seam - V1 | 272 |
| Three Pigs - V3 | 247 |
| Thrust - V7 | 136 |
| Thunder Thighs - V4 *(M. Dooley)* | 85 |
| Tick Arete - V2 | 77 |
| Tick Rock Traverse - V3 | 245 |
| Time Tunnel, The - V3 *(M. Dooley)* | 245 |
| Titanium Man Traverse - V5 | 223 |
| Titsma - V9 | 298 |
| Titty Fuck - V6 | 149 |
| Tombstone - V4 | 149 |
| Topanga Lieback - V0 | 276 |
| Torosa - V9 *(D. Gandy)* | 214 |
| Tortoise Traverse, The - V4 | 29 |
| Toss for it - V4 *(D. Fritz)* | 292 |
| Towers of The Teeth - V5 *(D. Gandy)* | 118 |
| Toxicodendron - V5 *(M. Dooley)* | 230 |
| Trailside #1 - VB | 213 |
| Trailside #2 - VB | 158 |
| Trash Compactor - V6 | 158 |
| Traverse - V3 | 109 |
| Traverse - V4 | 200 |
| Traverse - VB | 214 |
| Traverse or Submerse - V2 *(B. Leventhal)* | 137 |
| Traverserado - V6 *(S. Eaton)* | 73 |
| Tree Route | 92 |
| | 158 |

| | |
|---|---|
| Trouble Told - V4 | 209 |
| Turlock Face - V2 | 185 |
| Turlock Prow - V2 | 237 |
| Two Scoops - V2 | 85 |
| Two Worlds Collide - V9 | 86 |
| | 206 |
| | 89 |
| | 154 |
| | 85 |
| | 152 |
| | 158 |
| | 33 |
| | 77 |
| | 263 |

## U

| | |
|---|---|
| Ultraviolet - V10 *(B. Leventhal)* | 209 |
| Ummagumma - V4 *(J. Bachar)* | 185 |
| Ummagumma Crack - VB | 185 |
| Uncertainty Principle - V7 *(D. Gandy)* | 29 |
| Under the Gun - V3 | 106 |
| Undercling Traverse - V0 | 183 |
| Underdog - V2 | 103 |
| Unicorn Paradise - V0 | 31 |
| Unknown - V4 | 141 |
| Unnamed - V0 | 37 |
| Unnamed - V0 | 37 |
| Unnamed - V0 | 37 |
| Unnamed - V0 | 37 |
| Unnamed - V0 | 37 |
| Unnamed - V0 | 37 |
| Unnamed - V0 | 37 |
| Unnamed - V0 | 40 |
| Unnamed - V0 | 40 |
| Unnamed - V0 | 40 |
| Unnamed - V0 | 41 |
| Unnamed - V0 | 41 |
| Unnamed - V0 | 73 |
| Unnamed - V0 | 73 |
| Unnamed - V0 | 117 |
| Unnamed - V0 | 118 |
| Unnamed - V0 | 135 |
| Unnamed - V0 | 137 |
| Unnamed - V0 | 137 |
| Unnamed - V0 | 143 |
| Unnamed - V0 | 163 |
| Unnamed - V0 | 175 |
| Unnamed - V0 | 206 |
| Unnamed - V0 | 212 |
| Unnamed - V0 | 216 |
| Unnamed - V0 | 216 |
| Unnamed - V0 | 234 |
| Unnamed - V0 | 245 |
| Unnamed - V0 | 245 |
| Unnamed - V0 | 259 |
| Unnamed - V0 | 261 |
| Unnamed - V0 | 261 |
| Unnamed - V0 | 261 |
| Unnamed - V0 | 261 |
| Unnamed - V0 | 271 |
| Unnamed - V0 | 271 |
| Unnamed - V0 | 271 |
| Unnamed - V0 | 271 |
| Unnamed - V0 | 271 |
| Unnamed - V0 | 281 |
| Unnamed - V0 | 281 |
| Unnamed - V0 | 281 |
| Unnamed - V0 | 281 |
| Unnamed - V0 | 291 |

# INDEX - BY NAME

| | | | |
|---|---|---|---|
| named - V0 | 292 Unnamed - V2 | 276 | |
| named - V0 | 292 Unnamed - V2 | 276 | |
| named - V0 | 292 Unnamed - V2 | 276 | |
| named - V0 | 297 Unnamed - V2 | 282 | |
| named - V0 | 297 Unnamed - V2 | 285 | |
| named - V0 | 301 Unnamed - V2 | 287 | |
| named - V0 | 301 Unnamed - V2 | 287 | |
| named - V1 | 40 Unnamed - V2 | 294 | |
| named - V1 | 66 Unnamed - V2 | 298 | |
| named - V1 | 117 Unnamed - V2 | 301 | |
| named - V1 | 117 Unnamed - V3 | 66 | |
| named - V1 | 117 Unnamed - V3 | 66 | |
| named - V1 | 118 Unnamed - V3 | 137 | |
| named - V1 | 137 Unnamed - V3 | 143 | |
| named - V1 | 137 Unnamed - V3 | 149 | |
| named - V1 | 143 Unnamed - V3 | 149 | |
| named - V1 | 162 Unnamed - V3 | 189 | |
| named - V1 | 169 Unnamed - V3 | 189 | |
| named - V1 | 204 Unnamed - V3 | 189 | |
| named - V1 | 212 Unnamed - V3 | 204 | |
| named - V1 | 212 Unnamed - V3 | 247 | |
| named - V1 | 212 Unnamed - V3 | 255 | |
| named - V1 (B. Morham) | 234 Unnamed - V3 | 257 | |
| named - V1 | 247 Unnamed - V3 | 265 | |
| named - V1 | 257 Unnamed - V3 | 269 | |
| named - V1 | 257 Unnamed - V3 | 280 | |
| named - V1 | 257 Unnamed - V3 | 282 | |
| named - V1 | 257 Unnamed - V3 | 288 | |
| named - V1 | 260 Unnamed - V3 | 304 | |
| named - V1 | 265 Unnamed - V3 | 304 | |
| named - V1 | 268 Unnamed - V4 | 66 | |
| named - V1 | 268 Unnamed - V4 | 143 | |
| named - V1 | 278 Unnamed - V4 | 149 | |
| named - V1 | 278 Unnamed - V4 | 149 | |
| named - V1 | 280 Unnamed - V4 | 245 | |
| named - V1 | 282 Unnamed - V4 | 265 | |
| named - V1 | 285 Unnamed - V4 | 287 | |
| named - V1 | 294 Unnamed - V4 | 290 | |
| named - V1 | 297 Unnamed - V5 | 143 | |
| named - V1 | 298 Unnamed - V5 (J. Constine) | 202 | |
| named - V2 | 37 Unnamed - V5 | 275 | |
| named - V2 | 40 Unnamed - V5 | 282 | |
| named - V2 | 40 Unnamed - V5 | 297 | |
| named - V2 | 66 Unnamed - V6 | 298 | |
| named - V2 | 137 Unnamed - V7 (L. Carrera) | 203 | |
| named - V2 | 149 Unnamed - V7 | 278 | |
| named - V2 | 149 Unnamed - VB | 67 | |
| named - V2 | 162 Unnamed - VB | 136 | |
| named - V2 | 167 Unnamed - VB | 143 | |
| named - V2 | 167 Unnamed - VB | 152 | |
| named - V2 | 169 Unnamed - VB | 152 | |
| named - V2 | 169 Unnamed - VB | 152 | |
| named - V2 | 247 Unnamed - VB | 162 | |
| named - V2 | 259 Unnamed - VB | 163 | |
| named - V2 | 260 Unnamed - VB | 163 | |
| named - V2 | 262 Unnamed - VB | 163 | |
| named - V2 | 265 Unnamed - VB | 190 | |
| named - V2 | 269 Unnamed Traverse - V3 | 212 | |
| named - V2 | 269 Untold Story - V1 | 144 | |
| named - V2 | 274 Upper Bird Law Arete - V1 (M. Dooley) | 230 | |
| named - V2 | 274 Uprising, The - V6 | 103 | |

# LOS ANGELES COUNTY BOULDERING

## V

| | |
|---|---|
| V10 Traverse - V3 *(M. Dooley)* | 206 |
| V9 Dyno - V9 | 65 |
| Vaino Problem - V5 *(V. Kodas)* | 155 |
| Vaino Reach - V3 *(V. Kodas)* | 136 |
| Vaino's Dyno - V4 *(V. Kodas)* | 136 |
| Valdez - V1 | 155 |
| Vale of the Fell Beasts - V1 *(D. Gandy)* | 230 |
| Victory Arete - V4 | 267 |
| Vivarian - VB | 136 |

## W

| | |
|---|---|
| Wacky Huecos - V2 | 274 |
| Waiting, The - V7 *(W. Ureda)* | 31 |
| Warm Up Crack - V0 | 247 |
| Warm-up - VB | 65 |
| Warm-up - VB | 103 |
| Water Arete - V0 | 117 |
| Water Hazard - V3 *(M. Guardino)* | 73 |
| Water Traverse - V1 | 206 |
| Waugh Problem - V6 *(M. Waugh)* | 146 |
| Well, Do Ya Punk? - V6 | 282 |
| West Arete - VB | 135 |
| West Face - V0 | 174 |
| West Face - V2 | 135 |
| West Face - V2 | 171 |
| When the Levee Breaks - V2 *(B. Leventhal)* | 199 |
| Where Buddhahead's Dare - V4 | 278 |
| Whiplash Smile - V4 *(M. Guardino)* | 77 |
| Whirlpool Arete - V8 *(M. Dooley)* | 216 |
| Whirlpool Roof - V7 *(E. Gia)* | 216 |
| Whirlpool Warmup #1 - V0 | 216 |
| Whirlpool Warmup #2 - V0 | 216 |
| Why Follow the Fox – V0 *(T. Grim)* | 29 |
| Wills' Dyno - V9 | 268 |
| With All Due Respect - V6 | 263 |
| Womb With a View - V2 | 280 |

## X

| | |
|---|---|
| X Arete Left - VB | 97 |
| X Arete Right - V2 | 100 |
| X Problem - V3 *(J. Johnson)* | 100 |
| XXX - V7 *(D. Fritz)* | 100 |

## Y

| | |
|---|---|
| Y Crack - V1 | 260 |
| Yabo Arete - V6 *(J. Yablonski)* | 176 |
| Yabo Dyno - V8 | 191 |
| Yabo Mantle - V4 *(J. Yablonski)* | 136 |
| Yabo Roof - V3 *(J. Yablonski)* | 146 |
| Yard The Tool - V1 | 173 |
| Yardarm Crack, The - V2 | 304 |
| Yardarm, The - V3 | 304 |
| Yellow Belly - V6 *(S. Eaton)* | 97 |
| Yen - V5 | 272 |
| Yikes! - V8 *(D. Fritz)* | 77 |
| Your Everyday Junglist - V3 | 273 |

## Z

| | |
|---|---|
| Zach's Roof - V5 | 275 |
| Zodiac Direct - V3 | 206 |

# INDEX - BY GRADE

## VB

| | |
|---|---|
| Warm-up | 65 |
| South America Face | 66 |
| Unnamed | 67 |
| Sole Power | 85 |
| Sole Sister | 85 |
| Test Tube | 97 |
| X Arete Left | 97 |
| Warm-up | 103 |
| Adam's Rib | 104 |
| Easy 1 | 118 |
| Easy 2 | 118 |
| Easy 3 | 118 |
| Mantle | 118 |
| Descent Route | 126 |
| Casual Route | 126 |
| Jam Crack | 133 |
| West Arete | 135 |
| Unnamed | 136 |
| Vivarian | 136 |
| Descent Route | 136 |
| Nose Arete | 137 |
| Slant Rock Face Right | 137 |
| Slant Rock Face Center | 137 |
| Slant Rock Face Left | 137 |
| Traverse | 137 |
| Easy Face | 142 |
| Unnamed | 143 |
| Sierra Face | 143 |
| Silent Running | 144 |
| Lake, The | 144 |
| Downclimb | 144 |
| Southeast Arete | 145 |
| North Face | 145 |
| North Face Flake | 145 |
| Easy Money | 151 |
| Unnamed | 152 |
| Unnamed | 152 |
| Unnamed | 152 |
| Lake | 152 |
| Spiral Direct II | 154 |
| Chouinards Friction Problem | 155 |
| Chimney | 157 |
| Railside #1 | 158 |
| Railside #2 | 158 |
| Unnamed | 162 |
| Unnamed | 163 |
| Unnamed | 163 |
| Unnamed | 163 |
| Easy Face | 164 |
| Fat Problem | 168 |
| Light Problem | 168 |
| Northwest Face | 171 |
| Mozart's Traverse | 179 |
| Chmagumma Crack | 185 |
| No name | 190 |
| Mommy's Boy Left | 190 |
| Mommy's Boy Center | 190 |
| Downclimb | 206 |

| | |
|---|---|
| Middle Face | 214 |
| Purple Pyramid | 214 |
| Regular Route | 253 |
| Easy Face | 253 |
| Mr. Ed | 253 |

## V0

| | |
|---|---|
| Why Follow the Fox | 29 |
| Unicorn Paradise | 31 |
| Mantle Problem | 33 |
| Unnamed | 37 |
| Unnamed | 37 |
| Unnamed | 37 |
| Unnamed | 37 |
| Unnamed | 37 |
| Unnamed | 37 |
| Unnamed | 40 |
| Unnamed | 40 |
| Unnamed | 40 |
| Unnamed | 41 |
| Unnamed | 41 |
| Captain's Corner | 41 |
| Brett's Arete | 49 |
| Splitter Choss | 57 |
| Semi-Rad | 57 |
| Gutterball Left Face | 67 |
| Gutterball Middle Face | 67 |
| Lunker, The | 69 |
| Black Box | 69 |
| Unnamed | 73 |
| Unnamed | 73 |
| Hot Rod | 85 |
| Sugar Daddy | 85 |
| Sole Food | 85 |
| Pit Problem | 91 |
| Scoops | 91 |
| Mantle | 94 |
| Sharkfin | 106 |
| Landing Not Required | 107 |
| Luckyman | 109 |
| Even My Girlfriend Does It | 115 |
| Addiction | 115 |
| Water Arete | 117 |
| Unnamed | 117 |
| Unnamed | 118 |
| Little Traverse | 125 |
| Unnamed | 135 |
| North Face Pump Rock | 135 |
| Bob Kamps Face | 135 |
| Short Story | 135 |
| Unnamed | 137 |
| Unnamed | 137 |
| Mike's Up Problem | 142 |
| Black Roof | 142 |
| Unnamed | 143 |
| Bulge, The | 144 |
| Potholes Face #1 | 144 |
| Potholes Face #2 | 144 |

| | |
|---|---|
| Meatgrinder Mantle | 152 |
| Borealis | 154 |
| Shorty Shea | 163 |
| Unnamed | 163 |
| Critter Crack | 164 |
| Puggie | 166 |
| Arete | 167 |
| Pocket Face | 171 |
| Split Crack | 171 |
| Sleazy Tabloid | 172 |
| West Face | 174 |
| Face and Crack | 174 |
| Unnamed | 175 |
| Center Route | 175 |
| Southwest Corner | 175 |
| Texas Flake | 181 |
| Undercling Traverse | 183 |
| Flakes | 190 |
| Bowling Ball Problem, The | 198 |
| Headwaters Ramp | 198 |
| Mantle | 198 |
| Number Nine | 199 |
| Backside Warmup | 199 |
| Corner Pocket | 200 |
| Creekside #1 | 203 |
| Creekside #2 | 203 |
| Creekside #3 | 203 |
| Unnamed | 206 |
| Striated Pebble, The | 206 |
| Sandy Beach | 206 |
| Pebble Arete | 206 |
| Unnamed | 212 |
| Topanga Lieback | 214 |
| Dike Route | 214 |
| Whirlpool Warmup #1 | 216 |
| Whirlpool Warmup #2 | 216 |
| Unnamed | 216 |
| Unnamed | 216 |
| Fetal Alcohol Syndrome | 221 |
| Pebble Crack | 221 |
| Banny's Water Problem | 223 |
| Banny Face #1 | 223 |
| Banny Face #2 | 223 |
| Banny Face #3 | 223 |
| Banny Face #4 | 223 |
| Gaffer, The | 230 |
| Unnamed | 234 |
| Skypager | 235 |
| Neanderthal Safari | 237 |
| Blackbird Traverse | 239 |
| Hamburgler | 240 |
| Unnamed | 245 |
| Unnamed | 245 |
| Arete | 247 |
| Warm Up Crack | 247 |
| Slabby Face | 247 |
| Talk Dirty To Me | 253 |
| In The Name of the Father | 255 |
| Unnamed | 259 |
| Better Bold Than Old | 260 |
| Unnamed | 262 |

315

# LOS ANGELES COUNTY BOULDERING

| | | |
|---|---|---|
| Unnamed | 263 |
| Unnamed | 269 |
| Unnamed | 269 |
| Unnamed | 273 |
| Unnamed | 273 |
| Unnamed | 274 |
| Unnamed | 274 |
| Coulter Pine Cone Amnesia | 276 |
| Unnamed | 278 |
| Unnamed | 285 |
| Unnamed | 287 |
| Unnamed | 288 |
| Unnamed | 288 |
| Unnamed | 290 |
| Unnamed | 292 |
| Unnamed | 292 |
| Unnamed | 292 |
| Unnamed | 297 |
| Unnamed | 297 |
| Unnamed | 301 |
| Unnamed | 301 |

## V1

| | |
|---|---|
| Digging For Worms | 31 |
| Unnamed | 40 |
| Hollowman | 47 |
| Pocket Protector | 49 |
| Laundryroom Innuendo | 49 |
| Lost Keys Arete | 49 |
| Dangermouth | 52 |
| Glass Animals | 53 |
| Birds of Prey | 55 |
| Grimace | 55 |
| Unnamed | 66 |
| Anderson Problem | 69 |
| Niagara Arete | 69 |
| Street Legal | 85 |
| Lost In Space | 86 |
| Cleft Arete | 91 |
| Oasis Seam | 92 |
| Oasis Arete | 92 |
| Slide, The | 94 |
| Malibu Lieback | 96 |
| Slab | 100 |
| Shit Crystal | 103 |
| Better Than it Looks | 109 |
| 5.10 | 109 |
| Face #2 | 111 |
| Face #3 | 111 |
| Left of Arete | 115 |
| Unnamed | 117 |
| Unnamed | 117 |
| Unnamed | 117 |
| Unnamed | 118 |
| Unnamed | 118 |
| River Arete | 118 |
| Big Traverse | 125 |
| Jake's Face | 126 |
| Maggie's Face | 126 |
| Bleau's Face | 126 |

| | |
|---|---|
| Junky Roof | 126 |
| Crank Roof | 133 |
| Pump Arete | 135 |
| Slant Flake | 137 |
| Unnamed | 137 |
| Unnamed | 137 |
| Juan Carlo Problem | 143 |
| Unnamed | 143 |
| Untold Story | 144 |
| Pie Slice | 154 |
| Bold During | 154 |
| Slap | 155 |
| Valdez | 155 |
| Unnamed | 162 |
| Birdhole, The | 163 |
| Ozone Facto | 164 |
| Mantlelobotomy | 164 |
| Blocky | 165 |
| Down in the Hood | 167 |
| Unnamed | 169 |
| Blunt Arete | 169 |
| Southwest Corner | 171 |
| Reggae Route | 172 |
| Holy Shit | 172 |
| 5.10 Face | 172 |
| 5.9 Slab | 172 |
| Daily Circuit | 172 |
| Route Rustlin' | 173 |
| Yard The Tool | 173 |
| Alice in Slanderland | 173 |
| Carousel Edge | 175 |
| Maggie's Traverse | 180 |
| Texas Flake Arete | 181 |
| Arete | 183 |
| Crack Hand Traverse | 183 |
| Jaws | 190 |
| Jam Crack | 193 |
| Talibanny | 200 |
| Illuminati | 200 |
| Unnamed | 204 |
| Axle Problem | 205 |
| Muscle Beach | 206 |
| Hallucinogenic | 206 |
| Water Traverse | 206 |
| Hawaiian Face | 206 |
| Key Largo | 212 |
| Unnamed | 212 |
| Unnamed | 212 |
| Unnamed | 212 |
| Take Me to Your Litre | 213 |
| Banny's Bath | 223 |
| Forbidden Crop, The | 224 |
| Full Harvest | 224 |
| Vale of the Fell Beasts | 230 |
| Upper Bird Law Arete | 230 |
| Unnamed | 234 |
| Root Cellar, The | 235 |
| Neanderthal Crack | 237 |
| Discus | 240 |
| Center Face | 245 |
| Unnamed | 247 |

| | |
|---|---|
| Thin Seam | 247 |
| Credit Card Lover | 253 |
| Ed's Route | 253 |
| Unnamed | 257 |
| Unnamed | 257 |
| Unnamed | 257 |
| Unnamed | 257 |
| Y Crack | 260 |
| Unnamed | 260 |
| Unnamed | 265 |
| Unnamed | 268 |
| Unnamed | 268 |
| Thin Crack | 272 |
| Unnamed | 278 |
| Unnamed | 278 |
| Unnamed | 280 |
| Unnamed | 282 |
| Unnamed | 285 |
| Unnamed | 294 |
| Unnamed | 297 |
| Unnamed | 298 |

## V2

| | |
|---|---|
| and the Battle Begun | 29 |
| Life Is Short | 31 |
| Unnamed | 37 |
| Unnamed | 40 |
| Unnamed | 40 |
| Barndoor Mafia | 47 |
| Slop Arete | 47 |
| Lucky Strike | 49 |
| Neckbeard Aficionado | 52 |
| Apes Wall Prow | 62 |
| Unnamed | 66 |
| Prow | 66 |
| Gutterball | 67 |
| Niagara Fist | 69 |
| Traverse or Submerse | 73 |
| Crank Session or Swim Lesson | 74 |
| Celluloid Hero | 77 |
| Swim Wear | 77 |
| Blockhead Mantle | 85 |
| Pocketed Overhang | 86 |
| Pipe Dream | 86 |
| Cobble in a Dish | 86 |
| Man in the Moon | 86 |
| Street Legal | 86 |
| Barracuda | 89 |
| Flydaddy | 89 |
| Rock Lobster | 89 |
| Pit Arete | 91 |
| Jumping for Mantle | 92 |
| Jump Problem | 92 |
| DW | 96 |
| Fraidy Cat | 97 |
| Small with Big Consequences | 97 |
| X Arete Right | 100 |
| Beluga Whale | 100 |

# INDEX - BY GRADE

| | | | | | |
|---|---|---|---|---|---|
| Cross Step, The | 100 | Rollercoaster | 175 | | |
| Rebel Yell | 103 | Arete | 175 | **V3** | |
| Revolt | 103 | Quickstep | 179 | | |
| Power to the People | 103 | Seam | 181 | Lord of the Flies | 29 |
| Underdog | 103 | Sticky Fingers | 185 | Earthworm Jim | 29 |
| Lip Turn, The | 103 | Rodeo Style | 188 | Swig's Alcove | 33 |
| Small Fry | 103 | Right Arete | 190 | Roadside Traverse | 37 |
| Monos | 103 | Mommy's Boy Right | 190 | Bulletproof Wallets | 49 |
| Spencer's Prow | 103 | Pocket Traverse | 192 | Crosshairs | 52 |
| Lycra Boy | 104 | Face | 192 | Game of Death | 55 |
| Slap Happy Left | 104 | Niles Reardon Traverse | 193 | Cave Arete | 65 |
| Slap Happy Right | 105 | When the Levee Breaks | 199 | Bachar Ladder | 65 |
| Off The Tree | 110 | Garrett's Pit Problem | 200 | Unnamed | 66 |
| My Boy Bleau | 111 | Nude Beach | 206 | Unnamed | 66 |
| Baron Arete | 115 | Broken Flake | 208 | Water Hazard | 73 |
| Hypodermic | 115 | Stepping Stone | 209 | Kerwin Problem Right | 74 |
| Don't Move the Tree | 117 | Pan Am | 212 | Kerwin Problem Left | 74 |
| Red Spot | 118 | Large Kilo | 212 | Powerbeast | 77 |
| Cougar Snacks | 120 | Freebird | 212 | Powder Edge | 85 |
| Chossy Roof | 126 | Royal Traverse | 214 | Barely Legal | 85 |
| West Face | 135 | Rinse Cycle | 216 | Procrastinator | 86 |
| Southeast Corner | 136 | Dark Comedy | 216 | Druglord | 86 |
| 0-40 | 136 | Poprocks | 221 | Stuffed Leprohon | 89 |
| Northwest Face | 137 | Lower Bird Law Arete | 230 | Oasis | 91 |
| Dihedral Left | 137 | Hithlim | 230 | Bouldering for Dollars | 91 |
| Unnamed | 137 | Nananaloc | 234 | Crawfish and Chips | 91 |
| File Ups Traverse | 141 | Samuel Jackson | | Midsummer's Daydream | 92 |
| File Lieback | 141 | Memorial Arete | 237 | Prow, The | 94 |
| File Ups Mantle | 141 | Schism | 239 | Giant Step Unfold | 96 |
| Amphitheatre Traverse | 142 | Schism Direct | 240 | Spencer's Tree Problem | 96 |
| Corner, The | 144 | Tick Arete | 245 | LeProhon Press | 96 |
| Warlock Face | 144 | Unnamed | 247 | Arock Travers | 97 |
| Fiers | 145 | And The Son | 255 | Fear Factor | 97 |
| Foot and Mouth | 145 | Unnamed | 259 | X Problem | 100 |
| Warlock Prow | 145 | Unnamed | 260 | Mutiny | 103 |
| Corner | 148 | Unnamed | 262 | Tension | 103 |
| Two Scoops | 149 | Unnamed | 265 | El Diablo | 104 |
| Unnamed | 149 | Sloper Problem | 266 | Beelzebub | 104 |
| Unnamed | 149 | Unnamed | 269 | Lycra Man | 104 |
| Black Monday | 151 | Unnamed | 269 | Balancing Act | 104 |
| Black Frida | 151 | Unname | 274 | Slapshot | 105 |
| Ice | 152 | Wacky Huecos | 274 | Apparatus | 106 |
| Pete Skeleton | 157 | Unnamed | 274 | Island Boulder Traverse | 106 |
| Standard Route | 158 | Krusty The Clown | 274 | Naked Man Overboard | 106 |
| Renaissance Man | 158 | Unnamed | 276 | Under the Gun | 106 |
| Potholes Traverse | 161 | Unnamed | 276 | Intimidation | 107 |
| Unnamed | 162 | Unnamed | 276 | Islands in the Stream | 109 |
| Jack, The | 163 | In The Boughs of Hell | 280 | Face #1 | 111 |
| Hike to Nowhere | 164 | Womb With a View | 280 | Neanderthal | 115 |
| Edgeclipper | 165 | Unnamed | 282 | Squirrel Head Traverse | 117 |
| Jazzi Corner | 166 | Unnamed | 285 | Skidmarks | 118 |
| Unnamed | 167 | Bow Spirits | 285 | Martian's Landing Crack | 126 |
| Unnamed | 167 | Unnamed | 287 | Old Skool Cool | 126 |
| Johnny Bob Arete | 167 | Unnamed | 287 | Pump Rock Traverse | 135 |
| Unnamed | 169 | Abyss, The | 288 | Bootflake | 135 |
| Unnamed | 169 | Unnamed | 294 | Endo Boy | 135 |
| Matt's Face | 169 | Defroster, The | 294 | Three Pigs | 136 |
| Ouinard's Hole | 171 | Unnamed | 298 | Vaino Reach | 136 |
| Gus | 171 | Unnamed | 301 | Reach #2 | 137 |
| East Face | 171 | Gymnasium, The | 301 | Dihedral Right | 137 |
| | 175 | Yardarm Crack, The | 304 | | |

# LOS ANGELES COUNTY BOULDERING

| | | | | | | | |
|---|---|---|---|---|---|---|---|
| Unnamed | 137 | Separation Anxiety | 234 | Hieroglyphics | 117 | | |
| Pile Drive | 141 | Low End Theory | 235 | Toss for it | 118 | | |
| Gomer Pile | 141 | Caveman Squeeze | 237 | Nylon Boy | 135 | | |
| Amphitheatre Seam | 142 | Stone Age Struggle | 237 | Bootflake Direct | 135 | | |
| Unnamed | 143 | Tick Rock Traverse | 245 | Boulder 1 Traverse | 136 | | |
| Ramada | 145 | Unnamed | 247 | Real Yabo Mantle, The | 136 | | |
| Slime | 145 | Horse Farts | 253 | Vaino's Dyno | 136 | | |
| Over the Hoof | 145 | Do Me | 253 | Yabo Mantle | 136 | | |
| Bob Kamps Mantle | 145 | Ionizer | 253 | Leaping Lizard | 136 | | |
| Yabo Roof | 146 | And The Holy Spirit, Amen | 255 | Static Lizard | 136 | | |
| Hog Tied | 148 | Unnamed | 255 | Reach #1 | 136 | | |
| Crack, The | 149 | Unnamed | 257 | Sledgehammer | 141 | | |
| Crack Direct | 149 | Fish Arete | 260 | Scary Face | 141 | | |
| Scoopless | 149 | Unnamed | 265 | Unknown | 141 | | |
| Unnamed | 149 | Unnamed | 269 | Thaw Dyno | 142 | | |
| Unnamed | 149 | Techno Flash | 273 | Unnamed | 143 | | |
| Bull Market | 151 | Your Everyday Junglist | 273 | Crowd Pleaser | 146 | | |
| Corner the Market | 151 | Barndoor Aret | 273 | Ear, The | 148 | | |
| Lion's Head #1 | 151 | Fang, The | 274 | Inside Out | 148 | | |
| Sugar Pops | 152 | Unnamed | 280 | Pink Floyd | 149 | | |
| Spiral Traverse | 154 | Unnamed | 282 | Flying Circus | 149 | | |
| Spiral Direct | 154 | Unnamed | 288 | Unnamed | 149 | | |
| Split Decision | 157 | Seams Okay | 288 | Unnamed | 149 | | |
| Scrambled Eggs Traverse | 163 | Scrub Jay | 288 | Lion's Head #2 | 151 | | |
| Kodiak Corner | 164 | Pootchute, The | 294 | Johnson Arete | 155 | | |
| Eightball | 166 | Refrigerator, The | 294 | Pancake | 164 | | |
| Earthquake Face | 166 | Exterminator | 301 | Incubus | 166 | | |
| Guar Scar | 166 | Yardarm, The | 304 | Trouble Told | 172 | | |
| Kodas Corner | 167 | Unnamed | 304 | Slanderland | 172 | | |
| Radulator, The | 169 | Unnamed | 304 | Carousel Face | 175 | | |
| East Canyon Traverse | 169 | | | Largonaut | 176 | | |
| Buckets to Bag Dad | 171 | | | Ummagumma | 185 | | |
| Half Gram | 171 | ## V4 | | Roof Crack | 188 | | |
| Bush Doctor | 171 | | | Offwidth | 192 | | |
| Bad Press | 172 | Crawl Space | 31 | Headwaters Arete | 198 | | |
| Hand Crack | 179 | Ankle Grabber, The | 33 | Headwaters Traverse | 198 | | |
| Sculpture's Traverse | 180 | Rafiki's Tomb | 54 | Inbetweener, The | 199 | | |
| Flash Me | 185 | Grip Grand | 54 | Seam, The | 199 | | |
| Hein Flake | 185 | Little House on the Prairie | 57 | Purple Haze Traverse | 200 | | |
| Hawk, The | 188 | Han Shan Aret | 63 | Spencer's Roof | 200 | | |
| Unnamed | 189 | Kuan Chin Roof | 63 | Loaded Bunny | 204 | | |
| Unnamed | 189 | Recluse Roof | 65 | Chico's Locos Traverse | 205 | | |
| Unnamed | 189 | Unname | 66 | Lodestone | 205 | | |
| Left Arete | 190 | Kaptain Traverse | 69 | Purple Seedless | 209 | | |
| Maple Canyon Arete | 199 | Thunder Thighs | 77 | Katzy Corner | 209 | | |
| Traverse | 200 | Whiplash Smile | 77 | Colorado Arete | 212 | | |
| Halfway Roof | 203 | Lunge or Plunge | 77 | Black Knight Satellite | 213 | | |
| Unname | 204 | Kingpin | 86 | Traverse | 214 | | |
| Beach Face | 205 | Crawdaddy | 89 | Dimit's Bulge | 216 | | |
| Motherlode, The | 206 | Over Lord | 92 | Chicken Katzatore | 221 | | |
| Pebble Direct | 206 | Harder Than It Looks | 97 | Grovel, The | 222 | | |
| Zodiac Direct | 206 | Seamless | 100 | Constant Gardener, The | 230 | | |
| V10 Traverse | 206 | Flyboy | 103 | Gelirwen | 230 | | |
| Pungi Sticks | 208 | Diablo Overhang | 104 | Lizard King | 239 | | |
| Edge Traverse | 212 | Hungarian Traverse | 106 | EIEIO | 240 | | |
| Unnamed Traverse | 212 | Teflon | 106 | Unnamed | 245 | | |
| Pebble Beach | 214 | Face #4 | 111 | Slept Together | 253 | | |
| Mural | 216 | Recycler, The | 111 | Cheek to Cheek | 259 | | |
| Time Tunnel, The | 223 | Junky | 115 | Unnamed | 265 | | |
| Harvest Moon | 224 | Feel the Rush | 115 | Inner Freeway | 266 | | |
| Morigost | 230 | Railed Out | 115 | Crooked I | 266 | | |

# INDEX - BY GRADE

| | | | | | |
|---|---|---|---|---|---|
| Victory Arete | 267 | Mantle Problem | 175 | Frock Problem | 92 |
| Guru of the Alternative | 276 | North Face | 175 | A-Cups | 92 |
| Tombstone | 276 | Carousel Traverse | 175 | Desperado | 92 |
| Where Buddhahead's Dare | 278 | Router Bit | 176 | Traverserad | 92 |
| Daddy Longlegs | 287 | Sandlow Problem | 179 | Crocodile Rock | 94 |
| Unnamed | 287 | Sculpture's Eliminate | 180 | Yellow Belly | 97 |
| Unnamed | 290 | Hot Tuna | 181 | Uprising, The | 103 |
| Dragon Flake, The | 290 | Bachar Mantle | 181 | Buck and Aron's Dirt Track | 104 |
| Satellite Dish, The | 290 | Mickey Mouse | 181 | Trash Compactor | 109 |
| Tortoise Traverse, The | 292 | Reardon's Problem | 183 | Gold Rush | 115 |
| 150 lbs or Under | 294 | Face Problem | 185 | Shot's Fired | 117 |
| Door Magnet, The | 294 | Thimble of The Santa | | Goldfinger | 117 |
| Gaston Problem | 298 | Monicas, The | 198 | Say Goodnight | 135 |
| Crossfire | 301 | Gaslight Lantern | 199 | Angel Wings | 141 |
| | | Centerpiece, The | 199 | Real Crystal Ball Mantle, The | 145 |
| **V5** | | Soapstone Traverse | 199 | Waugh Problem | 146 |
| | | Unnamed | 202 | Apesma Rightt | 149 |
| It's Nyaaat Easy | 33 | Harmonica Lewinsky | 202 | Titty Fuck | 149 |
| Miniholland Traverse | 41 | Corkscrew | 212 | Cracksma | 149 |
| Paranoia | 47 | Toxicodendron | 213 | AG Pinch, The | 149 |
| Monkey Paw aka Kate Moss | 52 | DNS Roof | 221 | Sudden Impac | 154 |
| Madvilliany | 53 | Asteroid Belt | 221 | Johnson Problem | 157 |
| Panet of The Apes Traverse | 62 | Escape Plan, The | 223 | Snot Here aka Powerglide | 158 |
| Lai Mei Overhang | 62 | Towers of The Teeth | 230 | Font, The | 164 |
| Iceball | 63 | Mirkwood | 230 | Fritz Face | 165 |
| Le Coi | 85 | Gates of Moria | 230 | Microscope | 165 |
| 2 | 86 | Gollum | 230 | Plunger | 168 |
| Sacking of Rome, The | 86 | Sphere of Influence | 234 | Yabo Arete | 176 |
| Inball | 103 | John Travolta Memorial | | Cleared for Takeoff | 176 |
| Ode to the West Wind | 104 | Arete | 237 | Seam Stealer | 179 |
| Tête-à-Tête | 109 | Hamburger Decoy | 240 | Johnson Mantle | 185 |
| Recycle | 109 | Freeway Traverse | 266 | Guarglaphone | 185 |
| Boarded Regard | 110 | Beer Bet, The | 266 | Don't Touch the Banana | 191 |
| Squirrel Head Roof | 115 | Falcon, The | 267 | Fritz Arete | 205 |
| Earlobe, The | 115 | B1 Traverse | 268 | Psychic Over the Phone | 222 |
| Only Takes One Finger | 118 | Yen | 272 | Guerilla Growth | 224 |
| There's Something | | Pebble Pinching S.O.B. | 274 | Balam | 234 |
| in the Bushes | 120 | Unnamed | 275 | Helter Skelter | 239 |
| Aftershock | 135 | Zach's Roof | 275 | Helter Skelter Direct | 239 |
| Double Dyno | 135 | Great Curve, The | 276 | Big Man on Campus | 257 |
| Astoning | 135 | Springtime | 278 | Belgian Waffle Maker, The | 262 |
| Ghetto Bird | 141 | Bruce Lee Problem | 280 | With All Due Respect | 263 |
| Vince's Problem | 143 | Unnamed | 282 | Sharma Problem | 268 |
| Terra Traverse | 143 | Pumpernickel | 282 | El NinYo! | 273 |
| Unnamed | 143 | High Chaparral | 292 | Well, Do Ya Punk? | 282 |
| Nose Dive | 145 | Opposition Movement | 294 | Peanut, The | 287 |
| Master of Reality | 148 | Unnamed | 297 | Baby Rattlesnake | 288 |
| Masters Chamber | 148 | Pie Slice Traverse | 298 | Christmas Bonus | 297 |
| Expansion Chamber | 148 | Titanium Man Traverse | 298 | Unnamed | 298 |
| | 148 | Gutbuster | 298 | | |
| Desma Left | 149 | | | **V7** | |
| Darkside of the Moo | 155 | **V6** | | | |
| Sino Proble | 155 | | | Uncertainty Principle | 29 |
| Super Natural | 158 | Temporal Relativity | 29 | Waiting, The | 31 |
| Out More Often | 158 | Sandbox Traverse, The | 33 | If You Dare | 65 |
| Char Dyno aka | | Lost Keys of God | 49 | Spongebob | 73 |
| Dynamic Duo | 158 | Cave Direct | 65 | Full throttle | 85 |
| en | 165 | Purple Heart | 74 | Thrust | 85 |
| Scorpion | 165 | Full Powder | 85 | Terminator | 86 |
| Bite Me Not | 171 | Blow | 86 | Pablo Escobar | 86 |

319

# LOS ANGELES COUNTY BOULDERING

| | |
|---|---|
| XXX | 100 |
| Natural, The | 100 |
| Landing Not Included | 107 |
| Samsquatch | 115 |
| Save The Best for Last | 115 |
| Approach Shoes | 118 |
| Anderson/Johnson Traverse | 146 |
| Lynn Hill Problem | 158 |
| Old Man and the Point | 188 |
| Potato Chip | 191 |
| Cry Uncle | 193 |
| Unnamed | 203 |
| Kung Fu | 205 |
| Little Hercules | 208 |
| Sandlot | 208 |
| Purple Squeeze | 208 |
| Purple Prow | 208 |
| Whirlpool Roof | 216 |
| Ignoring the Obvious | 234 |
| Eriksson Problem, The | 257 |
| Arbor Day | 259 |
| Haiku | 260 |
| Unnamed | 278 |
| Mr. Skin | 285 |
| Sherman Variation | 292 |
| All This Time I Thought was an Actor | 298 |
| Teflon President | 301 |

## V8

| | |
|---|---|
| Black Fly Hell | 29 |
| Yikes! | 77 |
| Avalon | 94 |
| Lycraverse | 104 |
| Lycra Linkup | 104 |
| Lycrabolic | 104 |
| Roadkill | 115 |
| Leah | 120 |
| Low and Behold | 141 |
| Apesma Cente | 149 |
| Neal Kaptain's Horror | 149 |
| Night Train | 175 |
| Yabo Dyno | 191 |
| Purple Prow Direct | 209 |
| Whirlpool Arete | 216 |
| Spirit Animal | 230 |
| Sword of Damocles, The | 263 |
| Red Shouldered Hawk | 263 |
| Nothing but Sunshine | 287 |
| Orange Flambe | 297 |

## V9

| | |
|---|---|
| Torosa | 29 |
| V9 Dyno | 65 |
| Evenflow | 69 |
| Deadfinger | 74 |
| Captain Hook | 94 |
| No Honor Amongst Thieves | 115 |
| Roadkill Direct | 115 |
| Gato Cosmico | 118 |
| Crank Yanker | 133 |
| Titsma | 149 |
| Two Worlds Collide | 193 |
| Purple People Eater | 202 |
| Maelstrom | 216 |
| Hip Replacement | 216 |
| Wills' Dyno | 268 |

## V10

| | |
|---|---|
| Attack of The Ants | 29 |
| Cave Traverse | 65 |
| Huevos | 74 |
| Ed's Traverse | 149 |
| Ed's Direct | 149 |
| Cold Sushi | 181 |
| Ultraviolet | 209 |
| Blank Generation | 267 |

## V11

| | |
|---|---|
| Malibu Roof aka Chubbs | 65 |
| Fighting with Alligators | 188 |
| Purple Rain | 209 |

## V12

| | |
|---|---|
| Prow Sit, The | 94 |